APPLES OF GOLD IN
FILIGREES OF SILVER

New Perspectives: Jewish Life and Thought

BEREL LANG, *series editor*

Apples of Gold in Filigrees of Silver

*Jewish Writing in the Eye of
the Spanish Inquisition*

COLBERT I. NEPAULSINGH

Holmes & Meier
New York / London

Published in the United States of America 1995 by
Holmes & Meier Publishers, Inc.
160 Broadway
New York, NY 10038

Book design by Robert Sugar

This book has been printed on acid-free paper.

Library of Congress Cataloging-in-Publication Data

Nepaulsingh, Colbert I.
    Apples of gold in filigrees of silver : Jewish writing in the eye
of the Spanish Inquisition / Colbert I. Nepaulsingh.
      p.   cm. — (New perspectives)
    Includes bibliographical references and index.
    ISBN 0-8419-1358-7 (alk. paper). — ISBN 0-8419-1361-7 (pbk. :alk. paper)
    1. Spanish fiction—Classical period, 1500–1700—Jewish authors—
History and criticism. 2. Lazarillo de Tormes. 3. Abencerraje.
4. Montemayor, Jorge de, 1520?–1561. Siete libros de la Diana.
5. Religion and literature. 6. Inquisition—Spain. 7. Marranos—
Spain—Intellectual life. I. Title. II. Series: New perspectives
(Holmes & Meier).
PQ6066.N46 1995
863'.3098924—dc20   94-38056
                                                    CIP

Manufactured in the United States of America

For
Stephen Gilman

CONTENTS

PREFACE

THE STORY this book seeks to tell has not been told before. It is about how some writers in Spain, called *conversos* because they or their ancestors were converted to Christianity, defied the Spanish Inquisition. In their defiance, three of these daring writers produced masterpieces of world literature now widely credited with having contributed significantly to the development of the modern novel. *La vida de Lazarillo de Tormes y de sus fortunas y adversidades* is known as a prototype for the picaresque novel, *El Abencerraje y la hermosa Jarifa* for the Moorish novel, and *Los siete libros de la Diana* for the pastoral novel.

Especially since 1948, when Américo Castro defined Spain, in its essence, as the result of the coexistence of Christians, Moors, and Jews, scholars have debated with inconclusive fury whether or not the writers of these three works were conversos of Jewish descent. But these three texts themselves have never been persuaded to reveal the ways in which they affirmed their Jewishness at a time when, if it were exposed, they would have been burned as "mute heretics," and their authors would have been martyred at the stake.

To blind the agents of the Inquisition, the authors of these acts of defiance used a technique of subtle concealment based on Maimonides' explication of Proverbs 25:11, in which figurative meanings of greater value than the obvious ones are hidden like apples of gold beneath filigrees of silver. Among Jews, Polyphemos, the one-eyed Cyclops, was a perfect metaphor for the monoptic monocultural Spanish Inquisition. Affirming Jewishness in crafty writing, not just *under* but directly *in* the eye of the Inquisition, was tantamount to blinding the Inquisition heroically, just as Ulysses and his wandering comrades blinded Polyphemos. In this book's title, therefore, the term Jewish writing refers to acts in which Jewishness is brilliantly affirmed, though hidden of necessity under a Christian filigree. In other words, the pen became the pointed beam that blinded Polyphemos.

The writers of these works lived in sixteenth-century Spain. The story of their work is important because it is part of a longer story about a body of incredibly creative literature produced in Spain by Jews and conversos in an environment of mass persecution from 1391 onward.

Although conversos lived in Spain from the period shortly after the birth of Christianity, at no other time did these conversos produce works of literature that have delighted and puzzled the world as much as these texts. Of course, heroic acts of defiance have taken place in all cultures during all times of persecution. The story of each of these acts of heroism, like this story, is always worth repeating, if only because their ingenuity delights us at the same time that their heroism instructs us, fearfully, to defy the pitfalls of human cruelty.

This is by no means a story without application in our time. May it never ever happen, but imagine, for example, that some moral or immoral majority should gain control of your country and decree that all Jews leave or convert. (The Jews of Spain, too, never thought it would happen; even when it did, they remained confident that "the system" would permit them to arrive at some workable arrangement.) There would be, if that were to happen, many modes of heroic resistance, among the most satisfying of which would be some version of these masterpieces that immortalize their resistance in writing.

I came upon this story while I was writing another book about the history of Spanish literature (Nepaulsingh 1986). In that book, I discovered why certain Spanish masterpieces published after 1391 have baffled literary experts for over six hundred years: they are puzzling to critics because they are what I call *converso* texts, that is, texts written in such a way that Christians would understand them one way, while Jews would read the same words and understand them in a totally different, sometimes opposite, way.

I am convinced that the techniques for writing books like these were cultivated among Jews and conversos in Spain since the birth of Christianity. No one can be certain when Jews first settled in Spain. They may have gone there from elsewhere in the Mediterranean area at any time in Jewish history. We are certain, however, that Jewish settlements in Spain can be traced back at least to the times of the Roman Empire before the birth of Christianity (Baer I, 17). We can also be certain that with the birth of Christianity began the phenomenon of conversion from Judaism to Christianity so important to the history of humanity and central, in the context of this book, to the development of literary creativity.

Among the first of these Jewish converts to Christianity, of course, were the disciples of Jesus and many of the apostles of the early

Christian Church. Some of this early conversion might have taken place in Spain; the apostle Paul himself might have traveled to Spain, presumably to convert Spaniards—including Jews—to Christianity (Baer I, 16). It is quite feasible, therefore, that the people Spaniards later called *conversos* existed in Spain from the early days of Christianity, even though firm evidence of forced conversion on a large scale dates only from the fifth century, at the time of the invasion of Spain by the Visigoths around the year 414 (Baer I, 17).

Conversion, forced and voluntary, persisted in Spain with varying degrees of intensity until 1492, when Jews were ordered to leave Spain or convert; it persisted as well after 1492, when those Jews who chose to remain in Spain were pursued by the Inquisition. During all these times of periodic peace and frequent persecution, Jews and conversos in Spain certainly produced acts and writings of heroic defiance, but since I cannot hope to tell the whole story here, I must limit myself to the story of three little books that, all agree, changed the world of literature.

Because this is a story as much about how we all read as about how these texts were written, I begin, in Chapter 1, with a description of how I came to read these texts as I now do. In Chapter 2, I describe briefly the inquisitorial environment in Spain in which these three books were produced. Then, for those readers who always insist on contemporary evidence in theory for claims of quotidian practice, I explain, in Chapter 3, what theories coincide with the writing of converso texts. Next, in Chapters 4, 5, 6, and 7, I summarize the contents of each book and explain why I am convinced that each is a converso text. Because the *Lazarillo* is the most complex of these three works and, for that reason, perhaps, the most commented upon, I devote two chapters to it; first I explain how pre-reading *Lazarillo* recently, that is, thinking about it while reading other material, led me to discover some of its most important secrets; then I test this recent pre-reading against the text of *Lazarillo* itself, reading it carefully to see if the pre-reading was accurate. Finally, I try to explain why these books have held their secret for so long, and how we, as readers, can apply their lesson by being multicultural readers in a world where persecution is still rampant, and where inquisitions, commonly perceived to be institutions of the dark Middle Ages, go by other more modern-sounding names, like ethnic cleansing.

I recommend to all readers, even those who work with these little books constantly, that we reread them now together. The three texts are fewer than 250 printed pages altogether, and it will take no more than a few hours, at most, to read them; but I promise that those five or six hours might have been more poorly spent than in the reading of these beautiful masterpieces. To those who read English only, I recommend the translations by Harriet de Onís, John Esten Keller, and RoseAnna M. Mueller (listed in the Bibliography). I replace these translations with my own because this context demands a more literal rendition; and I always mean to cite, for the convenience of all readers, the number of the Spanish page first and then the English, like this: (29/12). The Spanish editions cited are by Alberto Blecua (1972) for *Lazarillo,* by Francisco López Estrada (1980) for *Abencerraje,* and by Francisco López Estrada (1962) for *Diana*.

Another version of this book exists, written for a small academic audience of Hispano-medievalists. It will never be published because before I could put finishing touches to it, I had robbed my patient family of so much irrecoverable time that it was clear that they deserved, at the very least, to be able to understand why. I decided, therefore, to rewrite the book for a larger audience of readers, among them, Marla, Jonathan, Rafael, and Ian, who have earned the right to read it.

There is, in my opinion, no need for modesty about this: Miriam Holmes and the staff at Holmes & Meier, especially Sheila Friedling, Katharine Turok, Maya Rao, Cornelia Wright, and others who have helped produce this book, run one of the best small publishing houses in the business. I thank them all for their professional contribution to this project.

Albany, New York
C. I. N.

APPLES OF GOLD IN
FILIGREES OF SILVER

CHAPTER 1

Life as a Text We Learn to Read: Point of Entry

for Mario J. Valdés

> *A second and higher aim of criticism is to engage in the critical*
> *dialogue with the tradition of literature as we have inherited*
> *it. . . . Most literary critics engage in this dialogue but only*
> *those who share their method of reading can contribute much*
> *to the reading of others. . . . The ethics of criticism are broadly*
> *defined as the activity of seeking the greater enrichment of the*
> *reader because of a mutual respect. Just as we can never have*
> *true dialogue without mutual respect, we will not have a genu-*
> *ine enrichment of the reading experience without respect for*
> *the reader.*
>
> —MARIO VALDÉS, *Shadows in the Cave*

W HEN WE say, as we often do, "I misread the situation," we mean
exactly that: that life is a text we learn to read. And yet we do not
always pay enough attention to how the texts we read affect our lives.
By paying attention I mean treating texts with the respect they deserve, not as "mute heretics," as the Spanish Inquisition tried to do.
Perhaps the most important part of learning how to treat life and
texts with respect is the constant practice of sharing how we read
with others, telling them as clearly as we know how what our point
of entry is, or, as the Afro-American vernacular wisely says, where
we are coming from. If I claim that we have not been reading these
three texts and others like them well for hundreds of years, I owe it
to my readers to explain exactly how I came to think so.

The point of entry for this study of three Spanish masterpieces is
a chapter of my earlier book, entitled *Towards a History of Literary
Composition in Medieval Spain*, published by the University of To-

1

ronto Press in 1986. Chapter 5 of that book begins to establish that the fifteenth-century Spanish masterpieces *Cárcel de Amor* (*Prison of Love*) by Diego de San Pedro and *Celestina* by Fernando de Rojas are *converso* texts, that is, texts that permit their meanings to be drastically altered depending on the perspective of the reader. That chapter was not about converso texts; it was about the Wheel of Fortune. But as I kept putting questions about the Wheel of Fortune to those two fifteenth-century masterpieces, *Cárcel de Amor* and *Celestina* kept telling me that they were converso texts, that they held one meaning for Christian readers and another quite different meaning for Jewish readers. Once I permitted myself to look at these texts from the perspective of different groups of readers in Spain, some sixteenth-century Spanish masterpieces, especially *Lazarillo*, *Abencerraje*, and *La Diana*, yielded new meaning and significance to me.

Once I saw these three sixteenth-century texts as I now do, I became very ambivalent about sharing my new readings in a published book: I wondered whether I would be training inquisitors to persecute writers in the future, or if I would be reminding subtle writers how to defy persecution in an inquisitorial environment. I was terrified by the thought that I would be exposing the secrets of these writers in a way that would have alarmed them. It was the quotation at the beginning of this chapter that helped me decide in favor of publishing my interpretations. I concluded that, if he knew about converso texts, and if he had realized to what extent we still live in an age of persecution, Salman Rushdie would have written a subtler book; sharing one's way of reading might steer another reader shy of stumbling blindly into pitfalls. Then again, blindness is a very stubborn thing to cure; insight is, miraculously, rare. For example, decades after Américo Castro gave us clues (about the multicultural makeup of Spain) that should have helped us read much better those texts composed in Spain before Cervantes (*Hacia Cervantes*), most of us, apparently, kept on reading in the same old ways. Let me use an example from my own experience.

In a course I taught on the history of the novel, there was an intelligent graduate student who seemed to grasp what I was saying, guardedly, about converso texts; she had also been a student in another graduate class that read the *Quixote* with me. Sometime after the end of the course on the novel, this student came to my office to inquire whether I would be willing to direct a thesis she was contemplating on a book called *Los amores de Clareo y Florisea* by Alonso Núñez de Reinoso. I agreed, provided that she would be willing to do a thorough annotated edition, as well as a literary analysis of the text. After the student had made several careful readings of the text and tried to make notes for every recondite word and allusion in it, she told me that she was ready to analyze the text as a converso text. I asked for textual evidence. She gave some clues, all of which relied on the fact that the author was converso. I told her that her evidence was insufficient, that evidence must come from the text itself; refusing to put ideas into her head about this particular text, which I had never read with her, I left her to her own resources.

Several painful visits later, I relented somewhat and asked her why, in her opinion, Núñez de Reinoso chose to describe the complexion of a beautiful woman in the book as "milk mixed with blood" (*leche con sangre mezclada*). The student, who happens to be Christian, replied correctly that milk mixed with blood would describe a nice rosy Renaissance complexion. I agreed, and waited a while in silence. It was only when I mentioned kosher laws that the candidate began to realize that the identical words that describe nice and rosy to a Christian also describe intolerable repulsion to an Orthodox Jew. This is a very transparent, hence risk-laden example, but it is opaque enough to elude most readers of Núñez' work, including this graduate student who was deliberately looking, like an inquisitor, for converso clues.

With regard to the claim of discovering converso texts, some may argue that all texts change their meaning and significance depending on the reader. While this is true, it is also true that all texts can be described along a spectrum, from those that attempt to limit the reader's capacity to derive more than one meaning from them to, at the other extreme, those that challenge, indeed defy, the reader to extract all the simultaneous meanings intended by the text. At the latter extreme, a converso text is culture-coded in such a way that its hidden meanings remain opaque to those who, if they were capable of discovering those hidden meanings, would persecute the author, while at the same time these opaque meanings are clear to a select group of subtle readers. Since it is possible to discuss all texts in terms of their intent to reveal or conceal, this book sought to describe how converso texts alone reveal and conceal.

For the term *converso* text, the word *converso* was borrowed from its condescending, discriminatory use in the history of Spain not to sanction that use, but to demonstrate how converso texts reverse condescension on the perpetrators, and triumphantly defy discrimination. Whereas inquisitors used the word *converso* to mean "New, hence inferior, Christian," or worse, "combustible Jew," converso texts reply to those hate-filled epithets by saying, not with reverse hatred but with self-affirming self-defense and consummate art, words to this effect: "You force your religion on me and think it superior; I will prove you wrong right under your watchful eye, letting you sense that I am mocking you; but your so-called superiority will never be capable of proving what your prejudiced instincts tell you. Burn me if you can crack the religious code I make glitter in my text!" Writing coded texts under persecution is not peculiar to Spain, but the production of converso texts in Spain can help us understand the universal phenomenon of producing coded texts in inquisitorial environments.

The historical context for what this book calls *converso* texts must begin in Spain, not with the establishment of the Inquisition in 1478, but at least with the riots throughout Spain in 1391, after which large numbers of Jews were converted to Christianity. More important, the geographical context for converso texts cannot be limited to the Iberian peninsula but must include everywhere that Jews were forced to wander after 1391—Europe, Africa, and, after 1492, the New World and the Philippines.

No single cause can be given for the massacre of Jews throughout Spain in 1391, but the events leading up to the massacre can best be understood against a background of economic chaos throughout Europe around 1348, the time of the Black Death. As frequently happens when economies turn sour, all Jews were blamed for the apparent financial success of a few among them. This was also a time of civil war in Spain, and all Jews were assumed to be on one side because a few influential Jews were on that side. The events are vividly described by Henry Charles Lea:

> When Pedro the Cruel ascended the throne of Castile, in 1350, the Jews might reasonably look forward to a prosperous future, but his reign in reality proved the turning-point of their fortunes. He surrounded himself with Jews and confided to them the protection of his person, while the rebellious faction, headed by Henry of Trastamara, his illegitimate brother, declared themselves the enemies of the [Jewish] race and used Pedro's favor for them as a political weapon. . . . When, in 1355, Henry of Trastamara and his brother, the Master of Santiago, entered Toledo to liberate Queen Blanche, who was confined in the alcázar, they sacked the smaller Judería [Jewish quarter] and slew its twelve hundred inmates without sparing sex or age. . . . When at length, in 1366, Henry led into Spain Bertrand de Guesclin and his hordes of Free Companions, the slaughter of the Jews was terrible. . . . Finally the fratricide at Montiel, in 1369, deprived the Jews of their protector and left Henry undisputed master of Castile. What they had to expect from him was indicated

> by his levying, June 6, 1369, within three months of his brother's murder, twenty thousand doblas of the Judería of Toledo and authorizing the sale at auction, not only of the property of the inmates, but of their persons into slavery, or their imprisonment in chains with starvation or torture, until the amount should be raised. . . . The condition existed for a catastrophe, and the man to precipitate it was not lacking. (Lea 1906, I, 101–03)

By the time Henry of Trastamara died in 1379, the man who was to precipitate the catastrophe of 1391 was already in action. His name was Ferrant Martínez, a fiery preacher and demagogue who, as archdeacon of a district in Seville called Ecija, had begun preaching hateful sermons against Jews in 1378. When the archbishop of Seville died in July 1390, Ferrant Martínez was promoted to a position of highest ecclesiastical power in Seville. On 9 June 1391, within one year of his promotion, Ferrant Martínez had whipped the people of Seville into a fanatical attack on the Jewish quarter. As Lea describes it:

> Few of its inhabitants escaped; the number of slain [in Seville alone] was estimated at four thousand and those of the survivors who did not succeed in fleeing only saved their lives by accepting baptism. . . . From Seville the flame spread through the kingdoms of Castile from shore to shore. In the paralysis of public authority, during the summer and early autumn of 1391, one city after another followed the example; the Juderías were sacked, the Jews who would not submit to baptism were slain, and fanaticism and cupidity held their orgies unchecked. (Lea 1906, I, 107)

In spite of the obvious traumatic nature of the events leading up to the massacre of 1391, however, those critics are absolutely right who would warn about the danger of making interpretative arguments "mutually permeable" (Round 1991). Are all Spanish texts composed since 1391 now to be considered converso? Of course not. All arguments in criticism must be validated initially and ultimately in the text itself, not in the mind of the critic. How does the critic begin to distinguish between ambivalence or simple double entendre and a converso text?

The first step, it seems to me, is to ignore the converso status (or lack of it) of the author—which preoccupied critics like Eugenio Asensio and Américo Castro—and concentrate, instead, on the converso status of the text. Converso authors do not always create converso texts; they are capable of other styles of composition. And writers who have studied converso texts, and who are not themselves conversos, can learn to compose converso texts, like, for example, the twentieth-century novelist Miguel de Unamuno who studied Diego de San Pedro's *Prison of Love* and the *Quixote* of Cervantes (see Nepaulsingh 1987).

Second, it is necessary to remember to ask not what the authors intended in these texts, but rather what the texts themselves intend. The difference between intentionality of the author and intentionality of the text has always been known (the Spanish Inquisition certainly made the distinction), but it is also frequently forgotten. We know, for example, that when children say they are hurt, they often mean not that they are in physical pain but that they need emotional attention (Hoy, 39). Spanish Inquisitors knew that they would not get very far if they were to cross-examine the authors of the three texts studied here; nor would we, if we were to resurrect the authors today. I remember Borges, whom a dear friend of mine called, in a book beautifully titled after Leo Strauss's, "the compleat solipsist," (Lang 1983, 202), vigorously denying that a passage in one of his works was indebted to Dante, when the debt was clear to all those in the audience who knew the two texts. The question of the author's intention is so complex that a reasonable person must admit that Borges might well have been right: polygenesis is as commonplace as borrowing. The intention of the text, on the other hand, almost always supersedes the intention of its author; when approached with appropriate respect, all texts, no matter how well or how poorly written, tell us things their authors left unwritten, though not necessarily unsaid.

Next, it is necessary to understand the kinds of environment that are conducive to the creation of converso texts. Persecution, for example, often yields what I call converso texts. What Leo Strauss has described in *Persecution and the Art of Writing* is worth citing here:

> Persecution . . . gives rise to a peculiar technique of writing, and therewith to a peculiar type of literature in which the truth about all crucial things is presented exclusively between the lines. That literature is addressed, not to all readers, but to trustworthy and intelligent readers only. It has all the advantages of private communication without having its greatest disadvantage—that it only reaches the writer's acquaintances. It has all the advantages of public communication without having its greatest disadvantage—capital punishment for the author. (p. 25)

Strauss was not speaking specifically about the same converso texts analyzed in this book, and it might be necessary to alter his definition slightly according to the context, but in essence his observation serves us well. Using Strauss as a point of entry, it becomes clear that a converso text must contain some element (word, image, or other reference) that is simultaneously unmistakably clear to some readers and almost entirely opaque to others; once this converso element is perceived, the entire work must yield a necessarily tortured meaning quite other than, even at times opposite to, the meaning more easily understood by most readers. The secret opacity and tortured meaning are vital, since a great deal is at stake, even life and death, but the enigma must not be trifling.

The ability to control clarity and opacity in a text is so developed in some Spanish masterpieces that one begins to suspect that it was not accidental, but was practiced on the basis of known theoretical premises forged from real life and applied at great risk. Equally important as the creation of converso texts, however, is their re-creation in the mind of optimal readers. The fact that converso texts have continued to keep their secrets hidden from readers for hundreds of years is a telling comment not simply on the artistry of those texts but also on the monocultural perspective of their readers. I use the word *monocultural* as an antonym of another new word—*multicultural*. It is curious that language and usage have long recognized the disadvantages of monoculture as it refers to agricultural dependence on a single crop; the obvious advantages of diversifying not just crops and investments but all of one's cultural experience have only recently been expressed in the broader, current significance of words such as *monocultural* and *multicultural*.

Since most readers are monocultural, it becomes the responsibility of those to whom multicultural perspectives come easily to share their mode of reading as widely as possible in order that all texts (from those that intend to be culture-bound along the entire spectrum to those that aim to be permeable among different cultures) might be created and re-created with greater sensitivity. It is for this reason also that I share with readers of this book in great detail the method that has led me to read these texts as converso texts. My intent is to suggest that, since there are clear and inseparable links between the acts of writing (or creating) and reading (or re-creating), then it becomes the responsibility of those who re-create what seem to be new readings to expose their basis for this new reading to detailed scrutiny. What has often been edited out of most traditional result-oriented criticism—that is, the *process* of criticism—is sometimes as important as what has been published.

The first requirement for breaking out of a monocultural mode of reading and writing, it seems to me, is the capacity to distance oneself at great length from one's own text; authors do not become totally without responsibility for what they write, but rather accept as fact that whatever one writes speaks for itself and only to a severely limited extent for its author.

During the last six years, I did not have the opportunity to reread the 1986 text that is the point of entry for this book, but from time to time, when the University of Toronto Press sent me book reviews, I was reminded of it. Frankly, as the years went by and the text receded farther from my consciousness, I understood less and less what the learned reviewers were talking about, and I remained only with the vague impression that the reviews were, on balance, good. Within the last few months, in preparation for this work, I reread the book in its entirety. I barely recognize myself in that 1986 text; it is too confident for my liking, too pert. And yet, since I would often forget who its author was, I found it hard to put down. When I read the reviews again, I found that those expert readers, too, had more or less the same ambivalent reaction toward the book: brash little book, but engaging. I was disappointed that, although there were serious criticisms about its methodology, no reviewer bothered to tear the book's central theses apart.

The review that delighted me most was written for *Speculum* by the late John K. Walsh of Berkeley. It is a beautiful review that parodies the racy style of my 1986 text. Walsh's exuberant praise can easily be turned to ridicule, depending on the perspective of the reader. When Walsh begins by stating, for example, that the book "is testimony to a splendid set of instincts," readers who like instinct in a critic will place emphasis on the adjective "splendid"; those who know that instinct should not interfere with scientific analysis would read the reviewer's opening sentence as ridicule. Regula Rohland de Langbehn, for example, is among the latter category of readers, and she states clearly, writing for the *Journal of Hispanic Philology*:

> It is Nepaulsingh who interprets allegorically: in hermeneutics this procedure is called "allegoresis," constituting an interpretation that is not based on the meaning of the interpreted text, but on fixed conceptions of the interpreter which he [sic] justifies by means of his [sic] analysis. It does not constitute a scientifically accepted procedure.

> (Es Nepaulsingh quien interpreta alegóricamente: en hermenéutica este proceder se denomina "allegoresis," constituyendo una interpretación que no se basa en el sentido del texto interpretado, sino en determinadas concepciones del intérprete que él justifica por medio de su análisis. No constituye un procedimiento científicamente aceptado.)

I agree with Rohland de Langbehn that the critic who cannot refrain from imposing an interpretation on a text should dispense with the pretense of criticism and, if capable, create a different work of art. Further, I found support for Rohland's view in one of Walsh's sentences, which says in its nonpraise perspective that "the subjectivity and unnerving verve in much of Nepaulsingh's writing is apt to strike a reader as indecent." Since I take pleasure in dismantling my own texts, I decided to reread the book, armed with this damaging accusation of subjective allegoresis from Rohland de Langbehn (and, in part only, from Walsh), with a view to selecting a better point of entry for this new book.

The 1986 book now took much longer to read, and the reading was more burdensome because I had always to refer, for every critical assertion, to the original text being criticized. This most recent reading was also twice as complex, at least: whereas at first there was a dialogue between me and each medieval text, there was now a four-way conversation among those medieval texts, the 1986 book, the reviews, and me, a different me in 1992. Whereas the 1986 text had said, "Frankly, I felt a little less than sane when I thought about talking to texts and having them talk back to me" (p. 5), I now felt positively schizophrenic. It did not help to hear texts tell me repeatedly, "But I told you that already many years ago. Don't you remember?" In brief, I found no major assertion in the 1986 book that was not supported by the medieval texts. At the end of my reading of the 1986 book, the favorite review that came to mind was the one by Anthony Cárdenas, especially the sentence that predicts, "The work will stand. Portions of it that may not will form detritus providing fertile ground for further scholarship."

I remained skeptical. Why will it stand? Am I not doing the same subjective thing all over again? Is this not circularity at its solipsistic worst?

As I struggled with these questions, I came up with three answers. First, the 1986 book's greatest strength is the risk it takes always to tell the reader, and so the writer, as honestly as possible, exactly where the point of entry is for every key discussion. This is what seems to make the 1986 book easy for some people to read, or, at least, easy to pick up again; and this is why this new text is repeating that risk of trying to explain in detail the precise point of entry.

Second, what often seems like subjectivity is better described as intersubjectivity. The 1986 book makes a serious attempt always to treat all critics, texts, and readers "as far as possible, as equals, and engage them in intersubjective dialogue in which there would be two

subjects, and not a perceptive critic as subject and an antiquated
petrified text as object" (p. 5). This new book has continued this
intersubjective approach, and it has made no assertion (I can summarize all major assertions here, if you insist, but they are many) that
cannot be reasonably agreed to by the other subject, that is, the texts
of *Lazarillo, Abencerraje,* or *La Diana.* The difference here is that
the 1986 book started with a method but with no premise, no agenda.
Here there seems to be a hypothesis at the outset, if not a conclusion,
namely that the *Lazarillo, Abencerraje,* and *La Diana* are converso
texts. What there is, in fact, at the point of entry to this new book,
is merely a heuristic assertion from chapter 5 of the 1986 book that
there *are* such things as converso texts; there is also a set of notes
written shortly after 1986, when a series of questions was respectfully
and appropriately posed to *Lazarillo, Abencerraje* and *La Diana,* that
led to the conclusion that they were indeed converso texts. I do not
now remember in detail what those notes say; I remember vaguely
only that the texts revealed themselves, for reasons worth explaining
in a book, to be converso.

Of course, if one does not like subjectivity of any kind, then intersubjectivity is worse than subjectivity: to those who spurn subjectivity, two subjects (or worse, this pretentious critic disguising himself
as two) are worse than one. On the other hand, is not objectivity—the
belief that one can take oneself out of it—merely an intersubjective
pretense? Is not intersubjectivity, in fact, a more reliable reflection
(than objectivity) of the human condition?

Many literary critics have an understandable fear of circularity. In
literature and in life, the expression "We're right back where we
started" usually explains an attempt perceived as having failed. In
fact, in my opinion, *we* never really get *right* back where we *started.*
The process of getting back changes us in such a way that a different
we must start again at a different point in time with a different text-
in-us. The expression "We've come full circle" often describes a more
productive experience than the expression "We're right back where
we started." This is why, whenever I enter a text with structural
analysis of part of it and exit with hermeneutic interpretation of the
whole from that part, and enter the structure and exit the whole
again and again, I am not really concerned whether or not this whole-
part-whole dynamic is best described as a subjective "circle" or an
objective "arch," as long as I enter always with mutual respect and
exit always without leaving the impression of having conquered or,
for that matter, of having been conquered. I have no rigid fear of

error or any imperialistic desire to be definitive. I care only that I leave an appropriately accurate record of the intersubjective dialogue.

As I did while preparing my 1986 book, I still find Hans-Georg Gadamer's *Truth and Method* a useful theoretical guide in my literary analysis, but it is amazing how, after a mere six years, a name like Gadamer can sound almost as antiquated in 1992 as René Wellek's sounded in 1986. If there is some postmodern equivalent of, some improvement on, Gadamer, I will at some appropriate point make necessary adjustments and abandonments. For the moment, my 1986 book and this one are sufficiently postmodern for my current taste.

When I ask myself whether to refer to literary theory of sixteenth-century Spain or of the twentieth century, I use the helpful distinction made by E. D. Hirsch in 1967 between meaning and significance. If I am after the *meaning* of a sixteenth-century Spanish text, I apply sixteenth-century Spanish literary theory contemporary with that text. If I am after the *significance* of a sixteenth-century text today or some time subsequent to its composition, I apply more recent critical theory. But we should not assume that twentieth-century literary theory (or twentieth-century life, for that matter) is superior to fifteenth- and sixteenth-century theory and life. The Spanish Inquisition, for example, clearly understood reader-response theory when it refused to admit the author to defend a text in person, on the grounds that the author would not be always present to make similar defenses to every reader. In fact, there are few, if any, current literary theories that were not known in medieval Spain, the land par excellence of biblical exegesis; that is the subject of another entire book not yet written, one like Susan Handelman's *Slayers of Moses*, but with special reference to Spain.

This distinction between meaning and significance cannot be avoided and should, instead, be embraced as a critical asset. The word *converso* in this book, for example, is loaded with denotative as well as emotional meaning, and many impatient readers will already have asked what, exactly, I mean by *converso*. But this is precisely the point: the concept *converso* cannot be petrified or frozen in the time that the word was coined; the concept has always existed and will always exist (all styles in all cultures at all times), and it is the work of the critic to elucidate its meaning, at the time of the word's coining, as well as its significance at other times.

A converso text is possible only if the composer of that text permits it to accommodate intersubjective meanings from different, even contrary, perspectives. An optimum reading enters a text with respect and engages it in intersubjective dialogue, the kind of dialogue that says, "All right, I see what you are doing, and I can do that too, but I don't have to be taken in by you or to relinquish my self, my subjectivity, entirely to your point of view." This relaxed engagement entices both subjects to be more self-revealing, to yield more of their secrets to each other than they would yield to someone or some other text that approached them with the disarming, ultimately false promise of unbiased objectivity. The written interpretation that results from such a reading does not speak for the critic, it speaks for itself; the critic remains too complex, as a human being, to be contained by any or all of his or her texts. Critics who read like this remain significantly free, if we choose, to denounce those texts, ours and others, whenever they attempt to imprison us in their meaning. Solipsism, on the other hand, is more like falling in love with one's own text, obliging oneself to defend its critical objectivity forever, for shame of having committed a minor error or major gaffe. With intersubjectivity, errors and gaffes are unembarrassingly welcome invitations to valid interpretation, significant oversights and undersights that lead to meaningful insights.

Indeed, whereas meaning is often forgotten, deemed dead, significance is vital. I must, in all honesty, report to my fellow Hispano-medievalists from whom this book also seeks consensus, that, from the upper administrative echelons of academia at which I have perched for the last four to six years, Hispano-medievalism often seemed, to most administrators, an easily dispensable luxury. Survival for Hispano-medievalism became feasible only when I engaged those powerful administrators in intersubjective dialogue about the forgotten meanings of 1492 and about the significance of those meanings in 1992 when even academic administrators were thinking about quincentennials. And when I ask myself today which publisher would risk issuing another title about texts as arcane, even if as resurrectible, as *Lazarillo,* I am tempted to desert this project as nice but not really necessary. If three sixteenth-century texts have been proved to be converso, so what?

On the other hand, is it not really a significant advancement in our understanding of ourselves if we can explain how words, the prime instruments of human communication, can be made to convey opposite meanings? Is that understanding not the kind of skill we need in order to avoid wars and other forms of self-destruction? Is not intersubjective converso subtlety a sine qua non in a viable, complex, multicultural world? Would conversos have been persecuted if Spanish Christians, Jews, and Moslems had succeeded, during their interminable debates, in engaging each other in intersubjective conversation? Is persecution a necessary incentive for the creation and comprehension of converso complexity? Is the mentality of the *conquistador*, the benevolent plunderer, the technically superior judge dispensing progress and interpretation from an even-handed objective stance, the only desirable approach to texts and to life?

In this book about converso texts, the caveat (about degenerating into meaningless relativism) that has been tossed at Gadamer by able-minded critics like Jürgen Habermas and E. D. Hirsch must be taken seriously. The fear is real that perceiving too many meanings is tanta-mount not simply to a blurring of the vision but to total blindness. To the linear episodic mind, one logical meaning must be processed sequentially after another logical meaning; parallel processing is viewed by sequential thinkers as a twentieth-century phenomenon, an anachronism in the interpretation of medieval and sixteenth-century Spanish texts. To jump from novels like *Lazarillo* and *La Diana* to poems like "To Cordoba" and "Polyphemos" in the same chapter is, to many sequential minds, to draw one's methodology serendipitously out of a mixed bag.

This book about converso texts must not be perceived to have resulted in what one reviewer of the 1986 book called "a mixed bag of critical perspectives at best" (Greenia). On the other hand, can there be no truth, no method in a mixed bag? Is not the human mind, medieval as well as modern, a mixed bag, a live multiple-processing organism, not just a parallel-processing machine? I am as much a mixed bag as Jorge de Montemayor, author of *La Diana*. The theoretical guide that makes my 1986 book a mixed bag full of Gadamer's truth and method is Mario Valdés. Valdés is a mixed bag full of precious theoretical gems. Valdés' mind was the mecca that brought people like Paul Ricoeur to Toronto in the era of Marshall McLuhan and Northrop Frye. Valdés' Darwinian idea that all "compo-nent elements—all of them—are at all times subject to diversifica-tion" made me see *all styles in all cultures at all times*, the concept that anchors my 1986 book away from meaningless relativism (Nepaul-singh 1986, 10; Valdés 1982, 165).

Another word about method: I may have given the impression that this book is being written because I "discovered" converso texts while working on my 1986 book, and like an undergraduate student who has just discovered symbolism and sees it everywhere, I proceeded to hunt down converso texts wherever I could find them. There was no such zealot's search. The notes to which I refer were not made while I was searching for converso texts; they were made as lecture notes for a class, not about converso texts, but about the origins of the novel. As I read *Lazarillo, Abencerraje,* and *La Diana* closely with that class, trying to show how *Lazarillo* is said to have fathered the picaresque novel, *Diana* mothered the pastoral novel, and *Abencerraje,* I suppose, brothered the Moorish novel, certain sections of those texts triggered quite another type of family question, already in the back of my mind, about converso texts; I proceeded with intersubjective respect and some skepticism to ask those sixteenth-century texts if they were converso. Now in 1992, I can see the question, then nameless and unformed, of a converso text germinating in my mind as I wrote "Lazaro's Fortune," published in 1980; germinating perhaps because, as people like Stephen Gilman kept reminding us, conversos had a special reason to think of themselves as victims of the goddess Fortune and her relentlessly constant wheel. The point is that, throughout my relationship with the texts analyzed in this book, I have remained, as all good readers remain, flexible and prepared for new experiences so that each reading would bring new significance for me.

The significance of these texts was clear to me because I could not exhaust their meanings at any single reading. The question remained: are these meanings intended by the texts or are they simply a normal result of the re-created experiences between reader and text over time? In other words, are these texts really converso, or am I cleverly imposing converso status on them? That question can be answered by the availability of theory, contemporary with the composition of these texts, that prescribes what the texts themselves practice. If the theory existed at the time the text was composed, chances are that the practice also existed. The contemporary theoretical base, which I suggest here can be found for converso texts in writers like Maimonides and Saint Paul, does not have to be a definitive source for converso texts but simply a part of the tradition in which the converso texts also were composed. Am I also imposing converso theory on Maimonides and Saint Paul? If I am clever enough to do that, then let the reader decide whether others before me in the fifteenth and sixteenth centuries were also clever enough to do the same.

CHAPTER 2

The Texts and Their Inquisitors

for George A. Shipley

THIS CHAPTER does not pretend to add new information about the Spanish Inquisition; for details on that topic, the general reader is referred to the learned volumes by Lea, Benassar, Alcalá, Pinto, and Kamen, listed in the Bibliography. Rather, the novelty of this chapter is that it provides, for the first time in the same space, a summary sketch of the Spanish Inquisition as a background against which to read texts like the *Lazarillo, Abencerraje,* and *La Diana* as converso texts.

The possible impact of the Spanish Inquisition on these texts has been discussed often before, especially regarding the converso status of their authors. Never, to my knowledge, have these texts been described as converso texts, that is, as texts deliberately coded to deceive and defy the Spanish Inquisition, which is why it is convenient to repeat a summary description of that institution here.

The Spanish Inquisition patterned itself after the institution that the Roman Catholic Church had developed throughout the Middle Ages for the purpose of expurgating whatever it deemed to be religious heresy. In Spain, the infrastructure of the Inquisition consisted of an Inquisitor General; a Supreme Council, over which he presided; and religious courts called tribunals, controlled by the Supreme Council. The tribunals were located in districts (first as many districts as necessary but quickly reduced in number to fifteen) throughout the Spanish peninsula.

The Inquisitor General and the members of the Supreme Council were appointed by the monarch. The question of who had greater authority, the Inquisitor General or the Council, was never really decided; it depended on the personality of the Inquisitor at a given period, and on the makeup of the Council. A strong-willed Inquisitor General, like Tomás de Torquemada, was able to defy the Supreme Council when necessary; after Torquemada's death, the Council, whose membership was not fixed in number, tended to be at least as powerful as the Inquisitor General.

The Inquisitor General and the Supreme Council used three main instruments to maintain control over the local tribunals: it served as an appellate body, especially for important cases decided (or left undecided) by the tribunal; it required monthly reports from the tribunals; and it sent plenipotentiary independent inspectors on periodic visits to examine all aspects of the working of a tribunal, including complaints against it from victims.

Early in the history of the Spanish Inquisition, the first Inquisitor General, Torquemada, defined a tribunal as consisting of two inquisitors, a legal adviser, a prosecuting officer, a police officer (*alguazil*), and as many petty officials as necessary (Lea 1906, II, 209). But this attempt to limit the number of officers failed. The number of inquisitors remained between one and three, but the number of people helping them ranged from as few as twenty-three to as many as one hundred and fifty. Positions as employees of the Inquisition were offered for sale in order to raise money, and in many instances these positions, once bought, were passed on to heirs, so that, over the years, entire Spanish families came to depend on the Inquisition as a source of income.

The inquisitors served as judges of the tribunal; one of their main functions when they were not hearing cases was to travel through towns and villages in order to ferret out denunciations against people. Legal advisers were deemed necessary when the inquisitors themselves were not versed in church law. The prosecuting officer was supposed to represent an improvement over the medieval papal inquisition, which lacked such an advocate, thus making the medieval inquisitor accuser and judge at the same time. Without serious advocacy for the defense, however, this Spanish improvement on the medieval institution was for procedural appearance only, not for justice, especially since the Spanish prosecutor took orders from the inquisitors (Lea 1906, II, 241–42; III, 42–50).

The police officer executed the orders of the tribunal; he made arrests, confiscated goods, and hired people to help him in these functions whenever necessary.

The petty officers were the ones whose increasing numbers swelled the official payroll of the Spanish Inquisition. Among them were messengers between the tribunal and the Supreme Council, court scribes, those who served summons on victims, those who ran the jails, physicians who examined prisoners before and after torture, barbers who doubled as surgeons, prison suppliers, chaplains, confessors, building maintenance personnel, and two or three lawyers for the defense who had to swear to denounce their clients if they found evidence against them (Lea 1906, III, 242–50).

The most feared employees of the Spanish Inquisition, however, were not the paid employees but some of those who volunteered their services without pay: the censors, the commissioners, the consultants, and, above all, the familiars. Three or four censors examined the preliminary evidence and judged whether or not it was sufficient to be submitted to the tribunal as an act of heresy; a great deal of the work of the censors was with printed material, especialy Bibles and books. The commissioners were appointed by the inquisitors to publish the decrees of the Inquisition and to assist in hearing evidence, but they often abused their limited authority and acted as inquisitors themselves. Consultants were legal experts hired on an ad hoc basis to help inquisitors and tribunals assess writings and sentence victims. Familiars were armed guards who received their name from the role they played in the medieval inquisition, when they protected inquisitors as though they were members of their family. In the Spanish Inquisition, repeated attempts were made to control the number of familiars, especially since records of those appointed as familiars were not carefully kept; since familiars were often exempt from punishment for criminal offenses, criminals were often freed when they claimed to be familiars of the Inquisition. The function of the familiar, in addition to protecting the inquisitors, was as an enforcer and a spy; their number kept increasing, not so much because of their function, however, but because the sale of the office of familiar was a source of revenue (Lea 1906, II, 263–84).

I have chosen to summarize the hierarchy of the Spanish Inquisition before describing how the institution affected books because the writer of a converso text was at risk of being denounced not just for writing heretical books but also for being a Judaizing converso. Conversos could be denounced because someone said they saw them wear their best clothes on Saturday, for example, or because they heard them say bad things about officials of the Inquisition, or for any of a long list of acts that were deemed to be typically Jewish. Once denounced, the inquisitors decided, with or without the advice of legal experts, whether the evidence in the denunciation constituted sufficient grounds for the arrest of the accused. If arrested, the property of the accused was confiscated until sentencing, the accused was held incommunicado, and the entire procedure was shrouded in absolute secrecy, especially the identity of the accuser and the unedited text of the accusation.

The accused was presumed guilty and was, in effect, impeded from establishing innocence. The inquisitors carefully edited the evidence, removing all possible traces of the identity of the witnesses, read the accusation section by section to the accused, and cross-examined the accused after each section was read. Then the lawyer for the accused was summoned and presented with the accusation and the response of the accused. The lawyer advised the accused, in the presence of the inquisitors, of the available options, which ranged from confession to calling witnesses who might counter the charges to pleading insanity or extenuating circumstances to accusing the inquisitor of partiality. If the accused failed to confess, and if the offense was considered serious enough, a confession was elicited by torture. Sentences included suspension (which meant leaving the case on file until more evidence was collected), abjuration, penance, whipping, public parade, gagging, the galleys, the wearing of a special robe (derived from the medieval sackcloth and ashes and called *sanbenito,* or "blessed sack"), the placing of these robes in churches with information about the identity of the wearer, denial of office to the victim's relatives, and death by fire at the stake or by strangulation before burning (Lea 1906, II, 470–586; III, 1–75, 93–194).

One important aspect of the inquisitorial procedure was the confession recorded during a period of grace. When a tribunal was opened a sermon was preached, and at the end of the sermon the inquisitors declared a period of grace for thirty or forty days, during which people were encouraged to make a full confession of their heresies in exchange for reduced punishment in the form of fines paid to the government to fight the Moors. Those confessing were not interrogated, but their words were carefully recorded and were later used against them if the confession was found to be incomplete (Lea 1906, II, 457–60). As I hope to show in the chapter on *Lazarillo,* it would have been inconceivable for Jewish or converso readers not to be reminded of this kind of confession as they read Lazaro's account of himself.

There can be little doubt that the inquisitorial environment described above had a profound effect on the three texts described in this book. The Spanish Inquisition was officially authorized by Pope

Sixtus IV in 1478; the first public punishments (*autos-da-fé*) were administered in Seville in 1481; and the first Spanish Grand Inquisitor, Torquemada, was appointed in 1483 (Alcalá, 1–2). The three texts we are discussing in this book were first printed, as far as we now know, in 1554 (*Lazarillo*), 1559 (*La Diana*), and 1561 (*Abencerraje*). The Spanish Inquisition was not officially dismantled in Spain before 1834 (although it had become irrelevant by the end of the 1700s), and was at the height of its repressive powers at the time the three texts appeared in print.

It is important to establish that, although these three texts were printed during the oppressive zenith of the Spanish Inquisition, they are part of a tradition of literature written by Spanish Jews and conversos at least from 1391. Some critics might argue that it is not proper to speak of "forced confession before Inquisitors" (Round, 317, Rohland de Langbehn, 180) before 1478 because the Inquisition was not authorized in Spain until that time.

The major historian of the Inquisition, Henry Charles Lea, argued that the papal Inquisition was very lax in Spain around 1478 because there was a "national aversion" toward it:

> in 1464, the Cortés assembled at Medina . . . complained of the great number of "*malos cristianos e sospechosos en la fé*" ["bad christians and religious suspects"], but the national aversion to the papal Inquisition still manifested itself and its introduction was not suggested. The archbishops and bishops were requested to set on foot a rigid investigation after heretics, and King Henry IV was asked to lend them aid, so that every suspected place might be thoroughly searched, and offenders brought to light, imprisoned, and punished. It was represented to the King that this would be to his advantage, as the confiscations would inure to the royal treasury, and he graciously expressed his assent; but the effort was resultless. (Lea 1887, II, 186)

Historians, including Jewish historians like Yitzhak Baer, often claim that efforts like the one described above originating at Medina, Spain, in 1464, were "resultless" because the Spaniards did not know how to institute a papal Inquisition:

> Espina listed all the types of heresy current in his day so as to convince the Spanish people that a well-organized and active Inquisition should be set up to deal with the conversos. With the same purpose in mind, he gave a detailed description of the canonical laws of the Inquisition, which seemed not to have been generally known in Castile. (Baer II, 286)

Baer is referring to a Franciscan monk by the name of Alfonso Espina who published a work called *Fortalitium Fidei* (*Fortress of*

the Faith), which was published in 1460. Baer is careful to say "not
. . . *generally* known" because clearly, if Espina, a Spaniard, knew
the laws for setting up a papal Inquisition well enough to write them
down in his book, then surely other Spaniards must have known
them. But the method of reasoning is still flawed: it is faulty to deduce
that the lack of an official papal Inquisition in Spain before 1478
means that there was little knowledge of official inquisitions there,
and that, therefore, Spanish texts written before 1480 could not imagine the environment of an official papal Inquisition. In fact, the documents cited prove otherwise.

Since Espina's *Fortalitium Fidei,* to which Baer is referring, was
published and widely discussed in Spain in 1460, then, surely, the
Spanish assembly to which Lea is referring, meeting at Medina four
years later in 1464, must have known exactly how to set up an official
papal Inquisition. This makes clear that the "national aversion to the
papal Inquisition" which Lea perceived cannot mean that the Spaniards could not imagine or describe what a real Inquisition was because there was none in their country for them to experience. It must
mean, on the contrary, that some Spanish writers, knowing full well
what a papal Inquisition was like elsewhere, chose to depict it in their
works so as to prevent what was already an inquisitorial environment
in their country from degenerating into a de facto legally instituted
fully functioning papal Inquisition in Spain.

Even before the establishment of a papal Inquisition, it was not
unheard of for a bishop in Spain to convene inquisitors to examine
and pass judgment on books that were deemed heretical; this was
what the bishops of Aragon did in 1297 and at several times in the
early 1300s (Lea 1887, III, 85, 613). With the advent of the printing
press, "It became a recognized rule that the person into whose hands
an heretical book might fall and who did not burn it at once or deliver
it within eight days to the bishop or inquisitor was held vehemently
suspect of heresy" (Lea 1887, III, 613). Indeed, this obligation to
denounce books as well as human beings reflect the Inquisition's
treatment of heterodox books as though they were people, mute heretics; books were denounced, arrested, examined in secret, sentenced,
and either expurgated or burned, leading one critic to refer to the
trial of a book as though it were the trial of a human being (Pinto
1983, 29).

The major differences between the trial of a book and that of a
person are instructive. First, whereas the accused person had at least
an impeded opportunity to respond to charges, an author was not
permitted to refute charges made against a book; the reasoning of

the Inquisition is that the reader of a book would not normally have the opportunity to question the author about its contents (Benassar, 256). This placed the burden of interpretation on the response of the reader rather than on the intent of the writer. The second major difference is that the Supreme Council did not permit the tribunals to pass final judgment on a book; the Council received the evidence submitted by the censors of the tribunal and made its own decision, often resubmitting the text to other censors before communicating a sentence to the tribunal for distribution in the community.

Over time, a system was devised to control the production and dissemination of books at all crucial stages of the publishing process. The secular arm of the government, not the Spanish Inquisition, controlled the printing of books before they were published by making licenses for printing, issued by designated officers of the state, mandatory. Once the book was printed the Inquisition's role began, although it could intervene before printing if an individual was found in possession of a manuscript deemed heretical. As of 7 September 1558, at about the time that *La Diana* might have been prepared for printing, the punishment for possession of a book condemned by the Inquisition, or for submitting a book for printing without permission, was death and confiscation of property (Lea 1906, III, 488). Lists of condemned books were issued by the Supreme Council and booksellers were required to display these lists at all times. Familiars were sent to raid bookstores and libraries for condemned books, and ships were boarded at key Spanish ports to control the importation and exportation of prohibited books.

Scholars can now point out with excellent hindsight that, although hundreds of thousands of people were burned at the stake by the Spanish Inquisition, no important writer of secular literature is known to be among those burned, so that the punishment was meted out to a greater degree on the books rather than on their writers. But there was no way for a writer, especially a writer in the sixteenth century, to know that the result of defying the Spanish Inquisition in secular writing would not be death by burning at the stake.

The history of Spanish literature in the vernacular Castilian language illustrates, in my opinion, that the risk taken by the authors of converso texts after 1492 was not fortuitous; it was a calculated and defiant reaction to their inquisitorial environment. Before 1391, Jewish and converso writers are not well represented as authors of major works in Castilian literature. There is the occasional converso, like Pedro Alfonso (born in 1062), who edited, in Latin, an anthology of anecdotes used by rabbis and priests as examples in their sermons, which were important to the development of the short-story form. There were Jewish poets who composed poems in Hebrew, around catchy vernacular expressions called *jarchas*, ornamental belt buckles; the poem is like a belt, with stanzas like jewels encrusted in it, and the *jarcha* cinches and releases the belt. But before 1391, the only major contribution to Castilian literature by a Jew or converso is the *Proverbios Morales*, over 600 four-line stanzas of proverbial sayings written around the middle of the fourteenth century by a rabbi named Shem Tov de Carrión.

Before 1391, the literatures of Spain reflect the fact that each of the country's three cultures was secure in its own linguistic environment. There was much creative interaction, of course, among cultures, but the Christians had their own literature in several Romance dialects, the Moors expressed themselves creatively in Arabic, the Jews had a vibrant corpus of secular writings in Hebrew—and in its literature, each cultural group described the others through stereotypes. There is evidence that even the *Proverbios Morales* of Shem Tov de Carrión, although written in Castilian, was intended mainly for a Jewish audience: the oldest surviving manuscript is written in Hebrew characters, and another manuscript dated 1492 consists of over 200 stanzas of the *Proverbios* written from memory by a man imprisoned for Judaizing by the Spanish Inquisition (Shem Tov de Carrión, *ii, iii;* López Grigera).

In 1391, it became clear that one of Spain's three cultures, the Christian, was going to insist on monoculture at the expense of the Jews and Moors. In that year Christians attacked Jews throughout Spain, killing thousands and forcing hundreds of thousands to convert to Catholicism. There had been attacks and forcible conversions before in Spain's history, but nothing like the riots of 1391. Lea describes 1391 as "a turning point in Spanish history. In the relations between the races of the Peninsula the old order of things was closed and the new order, which was to prove so benumbing to material and intellectual development, was about to open" (1906, I, 110). Baer describes the change this way: "A new type of apostate now emerged. Previously, Jewish apostates had entered their new faith as penitents, become monks, and appeared in public chiefly as persecutors of and missionaries to their former co-religionists. Now, change of religion was prompted by political considerations, serving as an 'admission ticket' to a world that was wholly secular and to a career in the civil and political bureaucracy" (II, 93–94).

This sea change in Spanish culture is clearly reflected in Castilian literature. Between 1391 and 1492, there was a marked increase in the number of conversos writing in Castilian, and their main purpose in writing also seems clear: they appeal directly to the Christian monarch of Spain to cure the political and religious ills of the country. For example, a converso poet, Alfonso de Baena, put together, in the first half of the fifteenth century, a collection of poems written mainly by conversos. Baena also wrote, perhaps for the collection, a long poem, addressed directly to the king, in which he describes Spain as an ailing country which would be healed if the king follows Baena's advice:

> Mighty King, according to the diagnosis
> your kingdom is ailing
> from such a great illness
> that it burns greater than a fire
> [if you do what this poem recommends]
> persecutions will cease
> as will the sighs of people,
> they will cease between their teeth
> from muttering curses,
> tribulations will cease,
> they will pray for your life,
> the church and its pardons,
> will cease from being overcrowded

> Alto Rey, segund la trama
> vuestro reyno está doliente
> de tan grande açidente
> que más arde que la llama
> . . .
> Çesarán persecuçiones
> e sospiros de las gentes,
> çesarán entre sus dientes
> que non lançen maldeçiones,
> çesarán tribulaçiones,
> rogarán por vuestra vida,
> çesará de ser corrida
> la eglesia e sus perdones

> (Baena III, 1171, 1220)

Another major poet, Juan de Mena, whose converso status many critics question, urges the king of Spain to "turn the rage, the rage against the Moors" ("La ira, la ira volved en los moros" [Mena, stanza 255]), as if to say, as some misguided Jews and conversos were wont to say, that the Moors, not the Jews, were the enemies of the Christians; misguided because prejudice and persecution ought not to be transferable from any oppressed group to another.

Then, after 1492, when it was clear that appeals to the monarch were not going to be effective, and when, in fact, the last Moorish stronghold, Granada, was conquered, the literary strategy changes from appeals to subtly coded defiance in a converso text. One of the first of these books of defiant protest was Diego de San Pedro's *Cárcel de Amor*, which first appeared in print in 1402 and was extremely popular in all of Europe, judging by the large number of editions and translations. It tells the story of a pair of lovers who are persecuted and sentenced to die because of the false testimony of an enemy. Although on the surface *Cárcel de Amor* tells an ordinary love story, it is told in the form of an apostolic Pauline epistle that parodies the Gospel of the Christian New Testament (Nepaulsingh 1986, 174–92); it also contains clues that lead Jewish readers to an interpretation of the work different from what Christian readers are apt to deduce.

A brief seven years after the appearance in print of *Cárcel de Amor*, one of the major masterpieces of Spanish literature was published: *Celestina* by Fernando de Rojas (1499). From a Christian perspective it tells the story of Calisto, a courtly lover who hires a go-between to help him seduce a young woman called Melibea, and leads himself, his lover, and the go-between to their untimely deaths. From a Jewish perspective, the same story is about an idolatrous young man who breaks the commandment to "have no other gods before me," and goes "whoring after other gods," calling Melibea his god and behaving, in effect, like Jews who worship the Christian Virgin Mary (Nepaulsingh 1986, 192–200).

The success of works like *Cárcel de Amor* and *Celestina* must have emboldened other Jewish and converso writers; both works escaped the censure of the Spanish Inquisition until 1632, when they were placed on the list of prohibited books. This must have sent a strong signal to writers of converso texts that it was possible to talk of simple stories about love and Fortune (the fortune of lovers) while sending carefully coded messages about religion and religious persecution.

As a cautionary measure, these works were probably first floated in manuscript anonymously; the first edition of *Cárcel de Amor* refers to the author in what seems to be an editorial addition to an earlier anonymous version of the work, and *Celestina* first appeared anonymously. But although the authors' names were not placed conspicuously where readers would normally expect to see them, the writer did conceal his name artistically elsewhere in the text. In *Cárcel* San Pedro makes references to the rock of St. Peter, and an acrostic with the author's name was added to the printed version of *Celestina* two years after its first printing. I say "printed version" because we will never know if the acrostic was part of earlier manuscript copies.

During the early years of the Spanish Inquisition, attention was given mainly to the censorship of Bibles and religious books. For example, in 1490, the Spanish Inquisition burned many Jewish Bibles and religious books, and "soon afterwards in Salamanca, it consigned to the flames in an *auto* some six thousand works on Judaism and sorcery" (Lea 1906, III, 480). In 1502, shortly after the publication of *Celestina* in 1499, the Spanish government decreed that "no book was to be printed, imported or exposed for sale without preliminary examination and licence" (Lea 1906, III, 481). With this new law, secular books were placed under greater scrutiny, although the primary emphasis remained on religious books.

By the time the *Lazarillo* appeared in print in 1554, the Spanish Inquisition's system of censorship was in full force. The *Lazarillo* was placed on the list of prohibited books in 1559; its anonymous author had chosen to abandon the theme of love and speak, instead, of the fortunes of a street-smart youth. From the time of its listing by the Inquisition in 1559, the *Lazarillo* was never again published in an unexpurgated edition in Spain until after the dismantling of the Spanish Inquisition in 1834. Expurgated editions appeared in Spain in 1573 and 1599, but the original version was published only abroad, in Antwerp, Milan, and Bérgamo. It is clear that some readers understood the *Lazarillo* as an attack on the Spanish Inquisition because, in 1620, a teacher of Spanish in Paris wrote a sequel to it in which the attacks against the Spanish Inquisition are not hidden. Some of this interest in *Lazarillo* outside of Spain is due, no doubt, to Spanish Jews expelled from Spain in 1492.

The Spanish Inquisition's list of prohibited books, issued in 1559, which banned the *Lazarillo,* also made illegal all books that appeared without the author's name. This is probably one reason why the *Abencerraje,* which had been circulating anonymously, begins to appear as part of works whose authors are named, like *La Diana* and a miscellany entitled *Inventario* (Inventory).

Despite the fact that the *Abencerraje* and *La Diana* were not prohibited by the Spanish Inquisition, they were not simply overlooked by an Inquisition that was preoccupied with Bibles and religious books and therefore lacked the resources or the will to examine them. We can be certain that they were scrutinized both by government censors before printing as well as by the censors of the Spanish Inquisition. They would have been examined carefully by government censors because anonymous books were highly suspect. They would have attracted the careful scrutiny of the Spanish Inquisition for four reasons at least. First, both books would have been suspect to the Spanish Inquisition as having something to do with conversos: an early printed version of the *Abencerraje* was dedicated to a rich Jewish converso, Jerónimo Jiménez de Embún, who was known to be a supporter of the Moorish converso cause against the Spanish Inquisition in Aragon (López Estrada, 48); and the author of *La Diana*, Jorge de Montemayor, was denounced in print as a Judaizing converso (López Estrada, *xiv*).

Second, after 1561, the *Abencerraje* was printed as part of *La Diana*, which was such a popular little book—the third most printed secular book of its time (Whinnom, 193)—that it was said, "There was not a house in which it was not read, a street in which its songs were not sung, nor a conversation in which its style was not praised, with every person, no matter how ranked they were, wanting to make private acquaintance of its author" (López Estrada, *xxx*).

Third, the Spanish Inquisition prohibited all of Montemayor's religious writings, but not *La Diana*, on its list of 1559, and again in 1583.

Fourth, *La Diana*, as well as Montemayor's religious writings, were prohibited by the Portuguese Inquisition (López Estrada, *xlv*) between 1581 and 1624, that is, during the time that Spain had occupied Portugal and was in control of Portuguese affairs (1580–1640); perhaps the Inquisition saw *La Diana* as more of a threat in Portugal where many Spanish Jews had fled after 1492 and where *La Diana* was even more widely read than in Spain.

In Spain and in Portugal, therefore, the Inquisition was after Jorge de Montemayor, author of *La Diana*, in which the *Abencerraje* was also printed. There is evidence, though not conclusive, that Montemayor himself acted as someone defiantly aware that the Inquisition was after him for his writings: he died not in Spain or in Portugal, but in Italy. He died defying the Inquisition, because we find him in Milan reissuing another edition of *La Diana*, shortly before his death in February 1561 (López Estrada, *xxxvi*, *lxxxvi*). The author of the *Lazarillo* would have been foolhardy to identify himself after his work was banned in 1559, but, as we shall see, he had concealed his name artistically in his text, and his artistry continued to defy the Spanish Inquisition for centuries.

CHAPTER 3

Apples of Gold in Filigrees of Silver

for Mrs. Stephanie Isser

T HE RELATIONSHIP between theory and practice is never easy to establish because it seems to be, almost always, a kind of chicken-and-egg question: Did someone describe a theory of converso texts based on the careful observation of how writers and other victims were defying the Spanish Inquisition, or was the theory invented first and later became the manual for defiance? In terms of the material presented in this chapter, Aristotle, Maimonides, and St. Paul derived their theories from the careful study of texts; but it is impossible to determine whether or not those texts themselves were created from the observation of everyday behavior. It is also impossible to determine whether the writers who seem to use Aristotelian, Maimonidean, or Pauline theories were drawn to these theories from what they saw happening around them, or whether the books of Aristotle, Maimonides, and St. Paul caused people to behave in accordance with the theories written in those books. Fortunately, it is seldom necessary to answer these questions; without claiming that theory caused practice or vice versa, this chapter will satisfy itself with citing theoretical texts that were available to converso writers, whether or not those writers knew and used them.

Converso texts, of course, are not the only ones that close off, through obscurity or ambivalence, their full meaning to some readers while at the same time they open themselves to subtle readers who know how to extract deeper and at times contrary meanings. One obvious way to understand this kind of closure and aperture is in

27

terms of sequels: a text may be considered closed if it does not lend itself readily to continuation, and it may be considered open if it does. For example, a well-known Spanish Christian writer of the fourteenth century, the Archpriest of Hita, puts an end to his *Book of Good Love* but declines to close it: "I shall put an end to my book, but I shall not close it" ("faré / punto a mi librete, mas non lo cerraré," 1626cd). He then invites competent people to add to it: "Whoever hears it, if they know how to compose poetry, may add more to it and emend whatever they wish to" ("Qualquier omne que l'oya, si bien trobar sopiere, /puede mas añedir e emendar lo que quisiere," 1629ab). On the other hand, another Spanish Christian writer of the same century, Don Juan Manuel, did not have much confidence in what might happen to a transmitted text and, as a consequence, he referred his readers to his original closed text, carefully housed in a monastery in Peñafiel. Additions and deletions, in Juan Manuel's judgment, would be detrimental to his important collection of short stories, the *Conde Lucanor* (Count Lucanor). Yet it is clear that Juan Manuel understood closure and aperture in a sense other than sequels, because in the second part of *Conde Lucanor* he explains that he wrote the first part in a plain open style so that everyone could understand, but that a dear friend of his (Don Jayme de Xerica) asked him to write more obscurely. It would be helpful, therefore, to distinguish between the ambiguity found in texts like the *Book of Good Love* and parts of the *Conde Lucanor* and that found in converso texts.

In texts like the *Book of Good Love*, ambiguity is based on what Aristotle describes as "the science of contraries [which] is said to be the same (for of contraries the one is no more an end than the other)" (*Topics* II, 3, 110b, 19–21; cited in Wolfson, 155–57). In the *Metaphysics* Aristotle wrote, "Every pair of contraries is to be examined by one and the same science, and in each pair one term is the privation of the other" (*Metaphysics* xi, 3, 106a, 18–20; in Wolfson, 156). In other words, in the pair of contraries good love/crazy love (*buen amor/loco amor*), good love (*buen amor*) is the privation of *loco amor*, and *loco amor* is the privation of *buen amor*, and both *buen amor* and the privation of *loco amor* lead to the same end. The point is that, in texts that are monocultural (that is, not meant to be interpreted differently by readers of more than one culture) ambiguity, as represented by contraries, is also monocultural; for example, good love is good Christian love, and bad love is bad love also in Christian terms. Converso texts, on the other hand, are multicultural, so that the same good love in one culture might be bad in another.

If the theoretical base for the aesthetic of contraries used by Juan

Ruiz, Juan Manuel, and other writers (like the Archpriest of Talavera, for example) is to be found in Aristotle and his commentators, the theoretical base for converso texts is found in the writings of Maimonides. In the introduction to his *Guide for the Perplexed,* Maimonides explains carefully how the same text can be made to convey opposite meanings. He warns the reader:

> Do not read superficially, lest you do me an injury, and derive no benefit for yourself. . . . The reader must, moreover, beware of raising objections to any of my statements, because it is very probable that he may understand my words to mean the exact opposite of what I intended to say. . . . There are seven causes of inconsistencies and contradictions to be met with in a literary work. . . . [The] Seventh cause: It is sometimes necessary to introduce such metaphysical matter as may partly be disclosed, but must partly be concealed; while, therefore, on one occasion the object which the author has in view may demand that the metaphysical problem be treated as solved in one way, it may be convenient on another occasion to treat it as solved in the opposite way. The author must endeavour, by concealing the fact as much as possible, to prevent the uneducated reader from perceiving the contradiction. (pp. 8, 9, 10)

Concealment of the contradiction leaves the text open to an opposite meaning accessible only to subtle readers.

Maimonides believed that his method was an imitation of biblical technique, and thus in accordance with God's Will:

> My object in adopting this arrangement is that the truths should be at one time apparent, and at another time concealed. Thus we shall not be in opposition to the Divine Will (from which it is wrong to deviate) which has withheld from the multitude the truths required for the knowledge of God, according to the Words, "The secret of the Lord is with them that fear Him" (Ps. 35:14). (p. 3)

One of the key biblical texts that Maimonides selected to explain his method in the *Guide* is Proverbs 25:11. Here is Maimonides' explanation, which I quote at length because of its beauty, clarity, and theoretical importance.

> The Wise King said, "A word fitly spoken is like apples of gold in vessels of silver" (Prov. 25:11). Hear the explanation of what he said: The word *maskiyyoth,* the Hebrew equivalent for "vessels," denotes "filigree network"—i.e., things in which there are very small apertures, such as are frequently wrought by silversmiths. They are called in Hebrew *maskiyyoth* (lit. "transpicuous," from the verb *sakah,* "he saw") because the eye penetrates through them. Thus Solomon meant

to say, "Just as apples of gold in silver filigree with small apertures, so is a word fitly spoken." See how beautifully the conditions of a good simile are described in this figure! It shows that in every word which has a double sense, a literal one and a figurative one, the plain meaning must be as valuable as silver, and the hidden meaning still more precious; so that the figurative meaning bears the same relations to the literal one as gold to silver. It is further necessary that the plain sense of the phrase shall give to those who consider it some notion of that which the figure represents. Just as a golden apple overlaid with a network of silver, when seen at a distance, or looked at superficially, is mistaken for a silver apple, but when a keen-sighted person looks at the object well, he will find what is within, and see that the apple is gold." (p. 6)

Maimonides' explanation of Proverbs 25:11 appears on the surface to be yet another variation of the medieval shell-and-kernel (*corteza / meollo*) commonplace, which placed greater value on things hidden subtly in the kernel than on those easier to reach on the outer shell. But Maimonides also recommends that his text not be read superficially, something that the *Lazarillo, Abencerraje,* and *La Diana* also strongly recommend. On closer scrutiny, Maimonides is describing what I call a converso text, that is, a text which to many readers seems to be silver, but which is, to those who know how to use its words "fitly spoken," something quite opposite—a text of gold.

To those readers who want to insist at this point that Maimonides is describing the interpretation of biblical texts, not the composition of literary texts, let me say that Maimonides' theory of biblical interpretation is rooted in his own experience with persecution in medieval Spain. It is worthwhile to refer here, once more, to the quotation from Leo Strauss, whose entire book, especially his third chapter on Maimonides, is crucial to the understanding of converso texts: persecution, in Strauss's opinion, is a rife environment for the creation of peculiarly coded texts directed to a wide public of superficial readers who are unlikely to perceive the deeper critical meanings accessible as private communication to only a few readers.

Strauss's description of the effect of persecution on literary composition reminds me of what the author of the converso text *Cárcel de Amor,* Diego de San Pedro, wrote to readers of another work of his: "But you, ladies, accept as service not what with roughness of expression I make public, but what by omission in its silencing I cover up" ("Pero vosotras, señoras, rescevid en servicio no lo que con rudeza en el dezir público, mas lo que por falta en el callar encubro"; *Arnalte y Lucinda,* 87). It also reminds me of how another converso, Alonso Núñez de Reinoso, described one of his works: "And so most of the

things in that story have a secret . . . because the truth is that I
wrote no word without first thinking what it meant underneath" ("Y
ansí todas las más cosas de aquella historia tienen secreto . . . porque
es verdad que ninguna palabra escrebí que primero no pensase lo
que debajo quería entender"; *Los amores de Clareo y Florisea*, 431).
But most of all, Strauss's conclusion reminds me of how Maimonides,
in his famous *Epistle on Martyrdom*, urged Spaniards to avoid persecution and death.

Maimonides was born in Cordoba in 1135, and shortly after his
birth, the Almohads who had seized control of certain parts of Spain
began forcing Jews to say in public that Mohammed was the prophet
of God. Those who refused to make this public declaration were
killed. Spanish Jews therefore sought the advice of their rabbis. One
rabbi ruled that Jews should choose to die, because if they did what
the Almohads demanded and then reverted in private to Judaism,
all their Judaic practices in private would be sinful. The family of
Maimonides fled to Fez and then to Egypt. Some scholars believe
that the father of Maimonides himself paid lip service to the Almohads, did what they wanted, and then fled at the earliest opportunity.
These scholars would probably maintain that Maimonides wrote his
Epistle on Martyrdom not merely to refute the other rabbi's harsh
ruling, but at the same time to defend his father's action. Whatever
his motives for composing the *Epistle on Martyrdom* around 1165,
it is clear that Maimonides' ruling on forced conversion became extremely relevant and popular in Spain, especially after the riots in
1391, when large numbers of Jews were faced with forced conversion.

Maimonides' ruling permits those whose life is in danger to pretend to convert, provided they avail themselves of the first opportunity to flee the country of oppression. In support of his arguments,
and in refutation of those of the harsh rabbi, Maimonides cites two
stories from Jewish tradition, one about Rabbi Meir who pretended
to eat pork to save his life, and the other, more to our purpose here,
about Rabbi Eliezer who was accused by the Romans of being a
Christian heretic, and whose "word fitly spoken" saved his life. I
quote from the *Epistle*:

> It is likewise well known that Rabbi Eliezer was seized for heresy,
> which is worse than idolatry. . . . Rabbi Eliezer was a celebrated
> scholar in the sciences. They inquired [of him]: "How can you be at
> your level of learning and still believe in religion?" He answered
> them in a way that made them believe that he adopted their doctrine,
> whereas in his reply he was really thinking of the true religion and
> no other. . . . The chief brought him to the capital and said to him:

"Say old man, is a person like you engaged in this stuff?" He replied:
"I have faith in the judge." The chief thought he meant him, whereas
he was really thinking of God, and the chief continued: "Rabbi, in
view of your having faith in me, I was indeed wondering, can he
possibly have been misled by such stuff? By God, you are free!"
(p. 20)

Once more Maimonides anchors his interpretation on the Bible
itself, and on the Psalms, this time Psalm 78:36: "Yet they deceived
Him with their speech, lied to Him with their words." Rabbi Eliezer's
"word fitly spoken," the one that saved his life, was *judge*. The text
was fitted like a silver filigree around this golden word so that the
average reader would be deceived into seeing one desirable superficial meaning and not the contradictory golden truth. The technique
is what Diego de San Pedro (1979, 173) called "conforming my words
with your thoughts" ("conformar mis palabras con vuestros pensa-
mientos"). The technique also explains that sentence in the prologue
to the *Lazarillo* that has puzzled all of us: "For it might well be that
someone who read them might just find something that would please,
and those who do not delve so deeply something that might delight
them" ("pues podría ser que alguno que las lea halle algo que le
agrade, y a los que no ahondaren tanto los deleite," 87/*xvii*); in other
words, those who do not dig deeply beneath the silver filigree might
just be amply entertained, but those who dig deeply to the golden
core will find the opposite of entertainment, they will find it hard, in
fact, to find anything at all that would please them. In the next chapter, I return in greater detail to this sentence and to two other related
sentences from *Lazarillo*'s prologue.

Shortly after 1391, the year in which many Jews were massacred
throughout Spain, the first translation of Maimonides' *Guide for the
Perplexed* was commissioned by Gomes Suárez de Figueroa, brother-
in-law of the Marqués de Santillana. The second book of the *Guide*
was translated in 1419, but Suárez died in 1429 before the entire
translation was completed by the converso Pedro de Toledo. The
complete translation, finished in 1432, made its way into Santillana's
library and has come down to us. Therefore, between 1391 and 1492,
the theoretical basis for what I call converso texts was available (and
highly relevant) in Spain, at least through Maimonides' *Guide*. Benzion Netanyahu documents that after 1391 the vast majority of rabbis
relied on Maimonides for guidance in what was happening to them.

Between 1391 and 1492, contacts between Jews and conversos
were severely curtailed, so that only a very clever few might have
had the luxury or the courage to learn to read well between Maimon-

ides' lines. But since the *Guide* reached Santillana's library after it was translated in 1432 and was surely available long after that to those who were perplexed at the persecution that had enveloped Christians, Moors, and Jews in Spain, we can be relatively certain that at least a few very clever writers availed themselves of Maimonides' advice. The tradition of converso texts thrives on the existence of only a daringly clever minority. Once texts like *Cárcel de Amor* and *Celestina* were composed, writers like Montemayor, Cervantes, and Góngora no longer needed direct access to Maimonides for assistance in composing converso texts.

If Maimonides provided the theoretical base for Jews and for those conversos who were secret Judaizers, conversos who were more accepting of Christianity took refuge in the rabbinical student and archetypical converso, one of the very founders and chief organizers of the early church—Saint Paul. Here it is important to remember that Maimonides was tapping into the tradition of the rulings of Jewish religious leaders about proper behavior in times of persecution, which goes back at least to the time of Moses. Saul, a student of Gamaliel, one of the most brilliant rabbis of his time, was obviously well versed in the rabbinical literature of persecution that, more than eleven hundred years later, served Maimonides so well. Saul tells us that he was one of the most zealous persecutors of Christians before his conversion (and name change) on the road to Damascus; he is said to have been present at and to have approved of the stoning of Stephen for blasphemy against Judaism. No serious rabbinical student would undertake to persecute Jews suspected of heresy unless he had studied the full consequences of his action; Paul had to be thoroughly acquainted with how heretics behaved and with what the interpretation of that behavior should mean. Therefore, it should come as no surprise to find the converso, Paul, now himself being persecuted for his acceptance of Christianity, giving expert advice to other conversos in his flock.

Paul's advice is not, like that of Maimonides, aimed always at deceiving; rather, if it does use deception, it would justify that means by the greater good of winning converts. In other words, Paul's method concentrates more on finding the kind of language and attitude that would eventually win converts through persuasion, not through the physical force he himself used as Saul. Maimonides, on the other hand, is not interested in converting (since Jews do not proselytize among non-Jews), but rather in giving advice about how to survive without committing heresy in the face of death. Despite the obvious difference between the two approaches, Paul's search for a common ground in communicating is as much at the very root of the creation of converso texts as is the advice of Maimonides.

To the Corinthians (I, 9:20–23; 10:31–33) Paul writes:

> To the Jews I became as a Jew, in order to win Jews; to those under the law I became as one under the law—though not being myself under the law—that I might win those under the law. To those outside the law I became as one outside the law—not being without law toward God but under the law of Christ—that I might win those outside the law. To the weak I became weak, that I might win the weak. I have become all things to all men, that I might by all means save some. . . . So whether you eat or drink, or whatever you do, do all to the glory of God. Give no offense to Jews or to Greeks or to the church of God, just as I try to please all men in everything I do, not seeking my own advantage, but that of many, that they may be saved.

In Spain, in the fifteenth and sixteenth centuries, whether the justification came from Paul or from Maimonides or from some other source, it seems clear that some persecuted writers felt the urgent need to create texts that would reconcile, or in some way reflect in varying degrees, the contrary texts and beliefs that were the source of oppression in their midst. Indeed, it would seem, to me, unnatural if artists did not attempt to create converso texts in times of persecution in Spain. In all three texts studied in this book, indirect reference is found to Maimonides' ideas about concealing from superficial readers; direct reference to Maimonides would, of course, have been ill-advised and perhaps deadly. Paul, on the other hand, was an acceptable source, and direct reference is found to his writings, in all three of the texts studied in this book.

CHAPTER 4

Pre-reading *Lazarillo*

for Jack Walsh

I<small>N THIS</small> chapter, I seek to establish how essential it is to pre-read texts properly. I choose *Lazarillo* to make this point because its very title announces it as a text aimed at teaching blind readers how to see more in the texts they read: apart from being a person's name, the word *lazarillo* also means a blindman's guide. By *pre-reading*, I mean the way we carry texts in our memory between different readings, including the way we think about texts when we read something else that reminds us about them; articles about texts, for example, make us remember and think about them. This should be called, correctly, pre-rereading, but I prefer pre-reading because, ideally, the next reading should be as fresh as if for the first time. First, I summarize from memory the contents of *Lazarillo*, referring to the written text only to copy key passages accurately. The summary is long partly for the convenience of those readers who do not know the text, but especially because I am inviting those who think they know the text well to read it in an entirely different way.

After the summary, because I want to discuss *Lazarillo* (in the next chapter) as a converso text, I think about the word *converso* while remembering an important phrase in *Lazarillo*. Next, I read and react to recent articles about *Lazarillo* in which certain portions of the text are copied and commented upon. Finally, in the last section of this chapter, I analyze *Lazarillo*'s full title in the light of what I have learned from this pre-reading. This procedure prepares me to read *Lazarillo* in a frame of mind that is wide open for new understanding.

The *Life of Lazarillo of Tormes and His (Mis)fortunes and Adver-*

sities (*La vida de Lazarillo de Tormes y de sus fortunas y adversidades*) is an autobiographical story told in a prologue and seven
chapters called "treatises" (*tratados*). In the prologue, the autobiographical narrator, Lazaro, addresses the entire story to someone
whom he calls by the respectful title "Your Grace" (*Vuestra Merced*).
Lazaro tells His Grace in the prologue that, since His Grace has
asked him in writing to send a written account with extensive details
about a certain matter or scandal, he, Lazaro, will tackle the request
not from the middle of things but from the very beginning, so that
His Grace might have a complete picture of Lazaro's personality.

Lazaro's prologue also contains three self-conscious sentences that
purport to explain why, in addition to His Grace's request, he is
writing his work. These sentences are deliberately enigmatic and are
written so as to be punctuated and understood in several different
ways. They are copied here because, as sentences characteristic of
the entire text, they help the reader understand why the rest of the
summary must be understood, in a Maimonidean sense, at superficial
as well as at deeper, contrary levels of meaning.

Lazaro opens the prologue by saying that he considers it "good
that things so remarkable and by chance unseen and unheard of
should come to the attention of many people and not be buried in
the sepulchre of oblivion, because it might well be that someone who
read them might find something that would please, and those who
do not delve so deeply something that would delight them" ("Yo por
bien tengo que cosas tan señaladas y por ventura nunca oídas ni vistas
vengan a noticia de muchos y no se entierren en la sepultura del
olvido, pues podría ser que alguno que las lea halle algo que le agrade,
y a los que no ahondaren tanto los deleite," 87/*xvii*). The superficial
sense of this passage (that the work is being published because it
might just contain something worthwhile, like all things do, good as
well as bad) is repeated in the following key enigmatic sentence in
the prologue:

And this ends up [suggesting] that nothing should be broken or dis-
carded as bad, unless it is very detestable, but it should be communicated to everybody, especially to those who are without prejudice
and are capable of deriving some benefit from it; because, if it were
not so, very few writers would write for one person alone, for this is
not done without effort.

Y esto para que ninguna cosa se debería romper, ni echar a mal, si
muy detestable no fuese, sino que a todos se comunicase, may-
ormente siendo sin perjuicio y pudiendo sacar della algún fructo;

porque, si así no fuese, muy pocos escribirían para uno solo, pues no se hace sin trabajo. (88/*xvii*)

The worthlessness of the work is again alluded to superficially in a third sentence that reads:

Confessing that I am no more a saint than my neighbors, it will not bother me if this unnaturally delivered trifle that I write in this gross style might be shared and enjoyed by all those who might find some pleasure in it, and may they see that a man [still] lives after so many misfortunes, perils, and adversities.

Confesando yo no ser más sancto que mis vecinos, desta nonada, que en este grosero estilo escribo, no me pesará que hayan parte y se huelguen con ello todos los que en ella algún gusto hallaren, y vean que vive un hombre con tantas fortunas, peligros y adversidades. (89/*xviii*)

It will take too much space to give the various correct punctuations and interpretations of these three sentences, but one example should suffice to demonstrate the multiple meanings of the entire text of the *Lazarillo*. The passage that means "but it should be communicated to everybody, especially to those who are without prejudice and are capable of deriving some [great] profit from it" also means "but it should be communicated to everybody, especially since it is harmless and capable of yielding some benefit [however little]." The latter superficial meaning denotes that the harmless trifling nature of the work makes it fitting for a vulgar universal audience; the former meaning, on the contrary, is that the work is written especially for the unbiased few who know how to derive its deeper value and true meaning.

Persistently, in a manner similar to the contrary meanings of this clause, there is, beyond the superficial filigree denoting worthlessness in each of these three sentences, the sense, available to those who read deeply, that, far from being worthless, the work is a rare gem, never heard or seen before, and appreciated only by the few who will find nothing at all pleasurable in it except its defiant mockery of those who dismiss it as a trifle. These sentences say, among their many intended meanings, that since it is so difficult to do, few writers intend words to have one superficial meaning for everybody and a deeper contrary meaning for a few select individuals. These, then, are the Maimonidean sentences of the prologue that guide the unperplexed, unblinded reader to the deeper meanings of the text; and the summary of the text that follows is best read with these three Maimonidean sentences in mind.

In each of the seven chapters, Lazaro tells about his experiences as a servant to different masters. In the first chapter, Lazaro begins by telling the story of his heritage from birth, leading up to how he came to serve his first master, a blind beggar. Lazaro explains that although his father was Tomé Gonzáles and his mother was Antona Pérez, he took the surname, Tormes, because he was born in the river by that name; his father ran a water mill in the river, and while his pregnant mother was at the mill one night, she entered into labor and gave birth to him there. When Lazaro was eight years old, his father was arrested for "bleeding" sacks of flour at the mill; he confessed and did not deny the accusation ("confesó y no negó", 92/1), for which he was prosecuted by the law. His father went to war against the Moors around that time and was killed. His widowed mother struggled to make a living cooking for students and doing laundry for stableboys. Working among the stablehands, Lazaro's mother met a black Moor and bore him a child. Her relationship with this Moor lasted until he was charged with stealing from the stables to support her. Lazaro was threatened and questioned by the authorities, and he confessed all he knew. Lazaro's mother was whipped, and the Moor was whipped and scalded with oil. Forbidden to have any further relationship with the Moor, Lazaro's mother went to work at an inn in order to support her two children.

While she was working at the inn, a blind beggar asked Lazaro's mother to let the boy serve him as a guide. The mother agreed, and Lazaro began life with his first master, the blind beggar, from whom Lazaro learned many hard lessons about life. For example, the first big lesson the blind man taught Lazarillo was to tell him to put his ear against a well-known stone sculpture of a bull in Salamanca. When Lazaro put his head close to the stone bull, the blind man pounded his head mercilessly into the sculpture, saying, "Fool, learn, because a blind man's helper must know a little more than the devil" ("Necio, aprende, que el mozo del ciego un punto ha de saber más que el diablo," 96/5). The blind man laughed a lot at this trick he played on his simple guide, and Lazaro wrote that this first key experience with his blind master woke him, in that very instant, from the simpleness in which he was asleep as a child ("en aquel instante desperté de la simpleza en que, como niño, dormido estaba," 96/5).

Lazarillo learns several more lessons like the stone bull, and he selects six among them to recount for His Grace. One of the six lessons focuses on bread as daily sustenance; because the miserly blind man locked his bread and valuables securely in a canvas bag, Lazaro was forced to survive by bleeding the bag and restitching the breach without being caught. A second lesson is about switching coins; Lazaro kept halfpennies and switched them for the pennies people gave the blind man. Lazaro's third selection is a lesson about wine. The blind man guarded his jug of wine constantly; Lazaro could only drink freely from the jug by inserting a long straw, and when his suspecting master started covering the mouth of the jug with his hand, Lazaro contrived to make a hole in the jug and cover it with wax, which he would remove when the time was opportune. The blind man discovered the wax; telling Lazaro nothing about his discovery, he let him settle to drink from the hole and then brought the jug crashing down on Lazaro's face, breaking several of his teeth and embedding shards of pottery in his flesh. He then washed Lazaro's wounds with the wine, reminding him with a biblical smile that what made him sick was curing him back to health. The fourth example is an accounting lesson using grapes: the blind man agrees to share a bunch of grapes with Lazaro provided that they would take turns eating one grape at a time. Shortly after they started eating, the blind man started eating two at a time; noticing this, Lazaro ate three at a time until the bunch was finished. The blind man then tells Lazaro that he was sure Lazaro cheated and ate three grapes at a time because Lazaro did not complain when the blind man ate two at a time. The fifth lesson is about a sausage: Lazaro ate a sausage the blind man was cooking and substituted a turnip in its place; to prove that Lazaro had eaten the sausage, the blind man stuck his nose down Lazaro's throat, causing Lazaro to vomit the sausage and return it to its rightful owner.

After these lessons, Lazaro was sufficiently well trained to be able to pay his blind master in kind. One rainy day, as they were about to cross a swollen stream, Lazarillo promises to take the blind man to a point where the stream is narrow enough for him to jump across it without having to wade through. Instead, Lazarillo positions the blind man carefully so that when he runs and jumps, he crashes into a stone pillar. Lazarillo laughs and abandons his blind master. These anecdotes and many others in the text read superficially like European tales strung together in a jestbook; I suggest a deeper meaning for them in the next chapter.

In chapter 2, Lazarillo serves a cleric who almost starves him to death by placing all the food, mostly bread, under lock and key in a chest. One day, Lazarillo obtains, from an itinerant tinsmith, a key that opens the chest; he proceeds to raid the cleric's food, leaving the impression that a house rat is the culprit. But one night, as Lazarillo slept with the duplicate key in his mouth, he started to snore, and the key made such a loud whistle in his mouth, that his master discovered the ruse; he beat Lazarillo mercilessly and fired him.

In chapter 3, Lazarillo serves a pretentious squire who claims to come from a noble family that has fallen on hard times. Every day the squire would leave his rented apartment early and not return until after dinner time; he would always claim to have eaten before coming home. Hunger led Lazarillo to seek out his own source of food, which, when he offered it, the squire would gobble up as a person who had not eaten for days. It turned out that Lazarillo had to feed this poor squire rather than the other way around, and, what is more, the squire had no money to pay the rent. When the landlord came to collect, the squire had already disappeared, leaving Lazarillo to face the police. The neighbors, from whom Lazarillo used to get food, supported his story, and Lazarillo barely escaped being imprisoned for the squire's debts.

The fourth chapter, only a short paragraph, was one of two chapters expunged by the Inquisition. It tells how the neighbors (really female hustlers, *mujercillas*) who saved him in chapter 3, took Lazarillo to a Mercedarian priest to whom they were so close that they called him a relative. Lazaro said he had to leave this master because he wore out a pair of shoes (a sexual cliché during the Middle Ages) in only eight days trying to keep up with him.

In chapter 5, Lazaro served a seller of papal bulls, or pardoner, who was a charlatan. He would scare innocent people, with lies and false miracles, into buying indulgences they did not need. When people were slow to buy these false indulgences, the pardoner had many techniques for persuading them, one of which, a dramatic ruse, Lazaro selects to tell in detail. The night before, the pardoner and his law officer would feign a fierce fight in which the officer would draw his sword and accuse the pardoner of selling false indulgences; the scene would attract the locals, spreading word in the town that the pardoner was selling phony indulgences. The next morning, before a packed audience in the local church, the officer would repeat his charge, and upright people in the church would attempt to eject the officer. The pardoner would insist that the officer be permitted to say as much as he liked. Then the pardoner would get down on his knees and implore God to bury him instantly if he was lying, and if the officer was lying to send some miraculous sign. At these words the officer would throw himself into a fit, foaming at the mouth as if possessed by a devil. Meanwhile the pardoner would remain on his knees transfixed, until some of the many men it took to subdue the bedeviled officer would implore the pardoner to do something about the officer who was apparently about to die. Then, the pardoner would say a solemn, moving prayer that he did not wish the officer to die but to repent and be pardoned; and, touching the officer with the text of an indulgence, the pardoner would heal him instantly. The exorcised law officer would then confess to the astonished public that he had lied and was made to lie by the devil. With this kind of evidence, many indulgences were easily sold. After four months Lazaro, disillusioned and no longer fooled by these ruses, left the bull seller.

In chapter 6, Lazaro served two masters. He helped a tambourine painter mix colors, suffering, he says "a thousand ills" (*mil males*); and he served a chaplain who equipped him with a mule, four jugs, and a whip and sent him around the city selling water for him. Business was so good that after four years, Lazaro was able to dress himself with fancy clothes and a sword, and give up the job.

In the seventh and final chapter, Lazaro again served two masters. First he worked for a police officer, but did not stay long with him because the job was dangerous. After he and his master were stoned and chased with sticks by some people (*retraídos*) who were seeking asylum in a church, Lazaro quit. Then Lazaro secured a job as town crier (*pregonero*), which he holds as he relates his story. As town crier, Lazaro comes to know the Archpriest of San Salvador, whom he describes as a servant and friend of His Grace. The Archpriest arranged for his servant to marry Lazaro, and also made it possible for the couple to rent a house next to his own. Town gossip got back to Lazaro that the arrangement was too cosy and that, in fact, his wife had given birth three times before he married her. But his wife and the Archpriest both denied this gossip so emphatically that Lazaro threatened to fight to the death anyone who impugned the honor of his wife.

For hundreds of years until very recently, most readers of the *Lazarillo* sympathized with Lazaro as an innocent little boy who has to learn life the hard way and is taken advantage of by adults. Most Hispanists of my generation and older can trace the time that the text of *Lazarillo* began to turn on them to their reading of L. J. Woodward's 1965 article. Woodward made modern readers realize that in spite of the tender diminutive (Lazar*illo* means something like "cute little Lazaro"), Lazaro is not an innocent little boy; he is a grown man who has been ordered by a superior to give a full account of a scandal involving an archpriest and, instead of explaining the scandal at length, chooses to tell a sob story about his hardships in life from birth. Obviously, as he aims to win His Grace's sympathy, Lazaro's own version of his life is not necessarily the whole truth.

I recall graphically the enlightened intellectual joy that article brought me, and when I teach the *Lazarillo* to undergraduates, I let them hang on as long as possible to their gullible emotional attachment to Lazaro before I introduce a post-Woodwardian reading of the text; (indeed, some undergraduates continue to believe Implacably in Lazaro even after Woodward). Maybe now it is a simple matter of intellectual joy; to the anonymous author of *Lazarillo*, it was a matter of life and death.

My interpretation of the *Lazarillo* took another dramatic turn as I was checking, out of curiosity, the meaning of *converso* in old Spanish dictionaries of the sixteenth and seventeenth centuries. The word *converso* is commonly defined in dictionaries of the Spanish language today as referring to Moors and Jews who were converted to Christianity. But if we define meaning as contemporaneous and synchronic, and significance as diachronic (Hirsch, 8), then today's meaning of *converso* masks a great deal of significance, modern as well as medieval. Among Jews today, for example, there is a wide spectrum of significance for the word *converso*, ranging from a faithful Jew who was forced to convert but never gave up the Jewish faith, to a faithful Christian who knows little or nothing about Judaism but who was persecuted by other Christians and their institutions simply because that person's ancestors were Jews; and between these poles of the spectrum, of course, there are numberless gradations and variations. Similarly, among Christians today, the word *converso* might range in significance from someone who saw the light of Christianity and perhaps is a better Christian than most because of the former experience with Judaism (like today's Jews for Jesus, for example), to someone who could never have been really Christian and who is always by definition suspect—again with many gradations between the extremes.

Twentieth-century significance of the word *converso* is clearly reflected in medieval and sixteenth-century meanings of the word: among medieval Jews, conversos were either *marranos,* a term which after 1380 (Netanyahu 1973, 59) was pejorative and meant swine; or *anusim,* a term which often connoted martyrdom, with many other terms between the pejorative and perfect poles. But, for the main purpose of this book, the most important meaning of the word *converso* is the one found in fifteenth- and sixteenth-century Christian writings, or better, in dictionaries approved by the Spanish Inquisition.

For example, the word *converso* exists in Sebastián de Covarrubias' *Treasury of the Castilian Language* (*Tesoro de la Lengua Castellana*), but not as a separate entry. To find the word *converso* in Covarrubias, one has to look under the homonymous word *confesso:*

> CONFESSO. One who is a descendant of Jewish or converso parents; and strictly speaking converso is coterminous with the conversion and return to the Catholic faith of those who had apostatized, who used to be called by another name "turncoats"; or we might say that *confesso* is the same as Jew, in so far as it comes from the Hebrew verb *iada*, which in the Hiphil conjugation means to confess . . . iehudi, iudaeus, from the same root.

> CONFESSO. El que deciende de padres judíos o conversos; y en rigor conversos vale tanto como convertirse y bolverse a la fé católica los que avían apostatado, que por otro nombre se llamavan tornadicos; o digamos que confesso es lo mismo que judío, por quanto viene del verbo hebreo . . . iada, que en la conjugación hiphil vale confiteri . . . iehudi, iudaeus, de la dicha rayz.

In other words, Covarrubias, an official consultant for the Spanish Inquisition (according to the Inquisition's censor, Pedro de Valencia), writing in the late sixteenth or early seventeenth century, knows the word *converso*, since he uses it in the definition cited above, but refuses to recognize that word except insofar as it means Jew. Covarrubias uses a curious form of scholarly (one is tempted to say Talmudic) etymology to make a political statement: all conversos are by definition and de rigueur Jews.

But Covarrubias' clever definition is itself a converso text. If one reads it as referring to all conversos, then it means that all conversos are Jews, including those who never converted themselves but whose ancestors converted from Judaism to Christianity; this is the meaning of "the person who is a descendant of Jewish or converso parents." But the rest of the definition (from "and strictly speaking," "y en rigor") means clearly that, strictly speaking, only a Judaizer, that is, one who reverts back to Judaism after converting to Christianity, is a converso; in other words, a sincere New Christian is not strictly speaking a converso, especially since that person, unlike his or her ancestors, may never have converted at all. There is, therefore, enough room in Covarrubias' subtle definition for all conversos: if one wanted to be Christian in public, one could use that part of the definition that says that only Judaizers are conversos; if one wanted to be Jewish in private and proud of it, one could hang on to the etymological thought that all so-called conversos are really Jews.

Although Covarrubias was writing between the late sixteenth and early seventeenth century, his etymology is not original. We learn from the authoritative eighteenth-century dictionary, the *Diccionario de Autoridades*, also approved by the Spanish Inquisition, that Covarrubias' definition of *converso/confesso* goes back as far as Antonio de Nebrija in the late fifteenth century:

> CONFESSO. Commonly used to refer to one who is a Jew by profession or race, who has converted; or one who has confessed in a trial to having Judaized. Covarr[ubias] in his Treasury and Nebrixa in his Vocabulary trace this meaning. Lat[in] *Neophyte* or *Convert from Judaism*. Pic[ára] Just[ina]. fol[io] 3: And I confess (if now from so much confessing they do not call me *confessa* [that is, converted Jewess]) that the hair which I have on me, hangs more on your word than on my head.

> CONFESSO. Comunmente llaman así al que es Judío de professión u de raza, que se ha convertido: u el que ha confessado en juicio haver judaizado. Trahenlo en este sentido Covarr. en su Thesoro y Nebrixa en su Vocabulario. Lat. *Neophytus*. vel *De Judaismo convictus, a, um*. Pic. Just. fol. 3. Y confiesso (si ya por tanto confessar no me llaman *confessa*) que los pelos que trahigo sobre mi, andan más sobre su palabra que sobre mi cabeza.

In this official eighteenth-century text, the word *converso* is not recognized at all, neither in the definition of *confesso* nor as a separate entry in its own right; officially, and for the Spanish Inquisition in the eighteenth century, conversos do not exist except as *confessos*, a synonym for Jews.

Thinking about *Lazarillo*, after having read the sixteenth-century definitions of *confesso* recently, made me realize that, in it, the word *confesso* is "a word fitly spoken." It is one key, perhaps *the* key, to a full reading of *Lazarillo:* it is the kind of simultaneously clear and opaque element required in a converso text. When Lazaro writes, referring to his father in chapter 1, "he confessed and did not deny" ("confessó, y no negó", 92/1); readers who see the verb *confessó* (meaning "he confessed") in this important passage are not likely to see the opaque noun *confesso*, meaning Jew or converso. Since the text takes pains to give its evangelical source ("for the Gospel calls them blessed"; "pues el Evangelio los llama bienaventurados"), Christian readers, especially, are not likely to see anything but the verb; even Jewish readers, like Stephen Gilman, who are looking for Judaizing clues remain blind to the noun *confesso* because attention is diverted immediately to what follows it. Gilman wrote, in 1972, a nine-page article on the New Testament text coupled in *Lazarillo* with "confessó y no negó," and although he is looking for Jewish clues he says nothing about the sixteenth-century dictionary meaning of *confesso,* choosing to concentrate instead, precisely as the text expects, on the words *persecución* and *justicia* (persecution, justice) in the same passage. And even when I saw the dictionary definitions of *confesso,* I did not see the term as key until I read the entire text again carefully. Part of the problem, of course, is that modern editions add an accent mark on the *o* and modernize the orthography by dropping an *s,* so that modern readers see "confesó" where the first readers of the text saw "confesso."

The most striking example, perhaps, of the opacity of the relationship in the text between the verb *confessó* and the noun *confesso* is the 1984 article by Manuel Ferrer-Chivite. Even though his purpose is to find *converso* underpinnings in the *Lazarillo* ("sustratos conversos en la creación de Lázaro de Tormes"), even though the noun *confesso* appears twice in the manuscript written by Sebastián de Horozco and cited by Ferrer-Chivite, even though Ferrer-Chivite himself isolates one of Horozco's phrases with the noun *confesso* in it, and even though Ferrer-Chivite's main critical method is semiologic linguistics, Ferrer-Chivite fails to see the noun *confesso* in *Lazarillo*'s text. Further, we can be certain that, even after they have read this chapter, many readers will refuse to see the noun *confesso,* meaning converted Jew, exactly as it does in the sixteenth- and seventeenth-century Spanish dictionaries and in the passage from the novel *Pícara Justina* ("if now after so much confessing they do not call me converted Jewess"; "si ya por tanto confessar no me llaman confessa").

But simply to see the word *Jew/confesso* in the text of any work is not to establish that that work is a converso text. Even the opacity of the word in *Lazarillo,* as opposed to its clarity in the *Pícara Justina,* is not evidence enough of the existence of a converso text. To validate the interpretation *confessó* as also meaning *confesso,* the careful reader must enter the text again intersubjectively and, fusing with all of it, ask, respectfully, if the *confessó/confesso* relationship holds for the work as a whole, and how. This is my application of what I understand by Heidegger's admonition "never to allow our forehaving, fore-sight, and fore-conception to be presented to us by fancies and popular conceptions, but rather to make the scientific theme secure by working out these fore-structures in terms of the things themselves" (in Gadamer, 236).

Already, even before one enters the text again, this approach is encouraged by the fact that we know from intelligent readers like

Wolfgang Iser and Peter Dunn that such a contrary phenomenon as converso texts is indeed possible, although these critics did not, of course, call the texts about which they were writing converso texts: "What is true for the individual reader is also true for the reading community. What a reader 'sees' in the text as a member of a particular cultural community will pass unrecognized by a reader in a different community" (Dunn 1989, 94). So that we already know that if we ask some readers, Victor García de la Concha (1972, 1981) for example, if *Lazarillo* is a Christian text, they will answer affirmatively and with impressive evidence; and if we ask another group of readers, Américo Castro or Stephen Gilman, for example, if the same *Lazarillo* is a Jewish or converso text, they will also answer in the affirmative with persuasive evidence, though not as much about the text itself as about its author.

But this is not enough: all these readings, though they yield meaning and significance in excess, are essentially suspect, because their approach was that of the conquering, inquisitorial mind; these readings have all tortured the text in some way. Critics who approach a text as *conquistadores* or as inquisitors will always capture its excesses, never its essence. Critics who approach and engage a text with intersubjective respect will not only experience essential meaning, but will also be in a position to add essential ontological significance to the experience of all readers. If this is true for critics, it might also be true for creators. If we ask how writers like the author of *Lazarillo* do what they do, one certain answer is intersubjectivity: these artists fuse with their material with such seamless respect that they are able to capture art not simply in its excess but also in its essence. And what is claimed here about conquering critics and subjected texts might very well be true about *conquistador*-type people and their victims.

For example, articles like my own 1980 piece on "Lazaro's Fortune" tend to sound triumphant and conquering; and articles like the recent one entitled "Lazarillo, La Ulixea y Anón" by Dalai Brenes Carrillo (1987), try to engage *Lazarillo* by asking, right at the outset, "Who is your author? Tell me or else." This approach to a text like *Lazarillo* is insensitive to the artistic necessity of anonymity of authorship; it may be appropriate to approach some texts with questions about the author, but in the case of texts like *Lazarillo,* the identity of the author was, at the time of composition, a matter of life and death. Likewise, articles like the one entitled "La intencionalidad religiosa del *Lazarillo*" seek to conquer *Lazarillo* with the opening interrogative threat, "What is your religion?"

Well-written converso texts will never yield their essential meaning to torture; they will, with intersubjectivity, yield tortured evidence of their full meaning and dynamic significance. It is quite
appropriate to anticipate that the evidence in a converso text, out of
vital life-or-death necessity, must be congenitally tortured; but it is
not appropriate (and, in fact, it is normally counterproductive) to
force a converso text to yield its twisted evidence. The reading must
respect the nature of the text, not mimic it with presumed superiority
and alleged objective remove or sleuthful distancing. There have always been readers, especially among Jews, who understand by instinct (without even having to think about it) what it is to embrace a
text, to be glad to see it, to feel it, to kiss it, to dance with it; there
have always been readers, especially in Islam, who with willing mystic
passivity let themselves be conquered entirely by a text, remaining
always and unconditionally prepared to die or kill for that text; and
there have always been readers, especially in the twentieth century,
who prefer to creep up on texts, to apprehend them with conquering
airs, or eat them up like the medieval biblical exegete, Pedro
Comestor, who got his name "Peter the Eater" because of his desire
to devour texts with insatiable comprehension.

Lazarillo is the kind of text that transmits fearsome delight. There
is so much incessant wordplay in *Lazarillo* that it should not be necessary to ask if the reading *confessó/confesso* can be validated in the
text and not just in the mind of the critic. When we ask the text if it
ever plays with the same word by shifting the accent from one syllable
to another, making a word accented normally on the last syllable
(*palabra aguda*, like *confessó*) become the same word with the accent
on the penultimate syllable (*palabra llana*, like *confesso*), the text
answers affirmatively. On the same page that the text tells us "confessó
y no negó," there is considerable play with the verb *tomar*, "to take,"
and the name *Tomé:* "A mí llaman Lázaro de Tormes, hijo de *Tomé*
Gonzáles y de Antona Pérez. . . . Mi nascimiento fue dentro del río
Tormes por la cual causa *tomé* el sobrenombre" ("They call me Lazaro
de Tormes, son of Thomas Gonzales and of Antona Perez. . . . My
birth took place in the river Tormes for which reason I took my
surname," 92/1). The verb *tomar* is chosen because it sounds both
like the name of the river (Tormes) and the name of the saint (Tomé);
but it is also chosen because it is the antonym of the verb *dar*, "to
give"; so that, in the clause "hijo de Tomé Gonzalez y de Antona
Perez," one reading will yield the same word *tomé* as a noun (meaning
Thomas), while another reading will elicit a contrary meaning by
shifting the accent on *tomé* from the last to the penultimate syllable,

in this case the first, and making the noun Thomas a verb in the imperative mood: "Take or keep the name Gonzalez and give (de) the name Perez to Antona (or the name Anton to Perez)." The original sixteenth-century text did not have modern accent marks and would have made sense both ways to readers of that time: son of Thomas Gonzalez and of Antona Perez in one sense, and son of ono person with a long surname (hence a long heritage) but simultaneously vulgar pedigree ("son of Thomas/I took-you take-Gonzalez-and-of-you give-Antona-Perez").

With this sort of wordplay, the text almost demands that *confesso*, a few lines later, be read both as a noun and as a verb. With appropriate punctuation the passage makes sense in two contrary meanings: "Por lo cual fue preso, y confesso y no nego ("For which he was taken prisoner, and he confessed and did not deny"), and "Por lo cual fue preso (y confesso) y no nego" ("For which he was a prisoner and a Jew, and he denied not"). The evidence for reading *confesso* as a noun is, as we should expect in a converso text, tortured, partly because the text is quoting the New Testament and there is no way to misquote the Bible and avoid the scrutiny of the Inquisition. But one should always read *Lazarillo* with at least three main texts at hand: a sixteenth-century dictionary, a Christian Bible, and a Hebrew Bible; one should also have one's ears, and eyes, recently cleaned in order to see and hear things never before heard and seen, exactly as the very first sentence of the text advises us (87/*xvii*).

To the ears of a sixteenth-century Spanish Christian, the phrase "confesso y no nego" is a quotation from the Bible meaning "he confessed and he denied not." But to the ears of sixteenth-century Spanish conversos and Jews the phrase was also a joke that could cost them their lives: it sounds like "a Jew and a fool for not denying it." To understand why this joke was and might still be today a matter of life and death, we need to recall its context in the Christian Bible:

> And this is the testimony of John, when the Jews sent priests and Levites from Jerusalem to ask him, "Who are you?" He confessed, he did not deny, but confessed, "I am not the Christ . . . but among you stands one whom you do not know, even he who comes after me. . . ." The next day he saw Jesus coming toward him, and he said: Behold, the Lamb of God, who takes away the sin of the world! This is he of whom I said, "After me comes a man who ranks before me for he was before me." (John 1:19–30)

The setting is inquisitorial. The inquisitors have been sent to find out if, as rumored, John the Baptist claims to be the Messiah. The punishment (rarely pronounced and executed) under Jewish law for falsely claiming to be the Messiah could have been death. John denies being the Messiah, but he also goes on to identify the Messiah, thus exposing Jesus to the death penalty. Later, in the sixteenth century, the setting is still inquisitorial but shifts from Jerusalem to Spain (all styles in all cultures at all times). In sixteenth-century Spain, to imply that John the Baptist was a Jew (*confesso*) was tantamount to inviting the scrutiny of the Inquisition; to imply that John the Baptist was a Jew and a foolish informer who did not know how to deny wisely while under interrogation by the Inquisition was, without a shadow of a doubt, to risk one's life.

In the Latin version of the text, the word *confessus* can be read both as a noun and as part of a verb ("Confessus est et non negavit"), giving clear biblical sanction to etymologists, like Nebrija and Covarrubias, who wanted authoritative precedent for reading *confessus* as a noun meaning Jew as well as a verb meaning "confessed." Seen in its ampler contextual meaning and in its significance from the first century to the sixteenth, the words *confesso y no negó* are vitally and fatally charged: they poke fun at Christians for their belief in foolish prophets and messiahs, at the Spanish Inquisition for accepting fools as witnesses, and they simultaneously poke fun at foolish Jews who do not know how to lie in order to save their own lives and the lives of others—"confesso, y! no negó!" ("Jew; and, he *didn't* deny it?! What a fool!"). An anonymous reader of this manuscript has suggested two other ways in which the joke might have been heard: "Confesso, y non ego," that is, "He is the Jew, and not I"; and the same reader also suggests that people like Lazaro's father are silly to think that confessing and not denying would make them as guiltless and as saintly as John the Baptist in the eyes of the Spanish Inquisition. The concept *confessó/confesso*, therefore, and the jokes about the biblical text that uses that word, encourage us to continue our intersubjective dialogue with the text of *Lazarillo* about its converso status.

We have claimed that the text of *Lazarillo* will yield its excesses but never its essence to the inquisitorial conqueror critic. The 1987 article by Brenes Carrillo provides an unusually good opportunity to test that claim, while at the same time advancing our pre-reading of *Lazarillo* as a *confessó/confesso* text. Brenes Carrillo (who is, at the time I write this, a bright young man of ninety and whose article is the best on the subject in the last decade, in my opinion) leaves the text of *Lazarillo* in triumph, having tortured the text to yield impressive evidence that its author is Gonzalo Pérez, translator of Homer's *Ulysses*. We must be careful now to enter Brenes Carrillo's text with the respect it deserves: it teaches us a lot, even if at times by negative example, about the text of *Lazarillo*. Let us then accept as true everything that Brenes Carrillo claims, not for the sake of argument, but out of respect, and for the sake of intersubjective dialogue with Brenes Carrillo's text.

If Gonzalo Pérez, translator of Homer's *Ulysses* (*Ulixea*), is the author of *Lazarillo*, does that mean that *Lazarillo* is not a *confessó/confesso* text? No. It means, on the contrary, that we have more evidence for the *confessó/confesso* status of *Lazarillo*. Here is one of many passages from *Ulixea* that Brenes Carrillo uses to prove his claim:

Tell me, gentle Muse, about that man
who wandered as a pilgrim over many lands and
nations learning of their ways of life and
customs: who, once the destruction of sacred
Troy was complete, sailed over the sea for
such a long time, suffering many travails and
stormy misfortunos.

Dime de aquel varon suave Musa,
Que por diversas tierras, y naciones
Anduvo peregrino, conociendo
Sus vidas y costumbres: acabada
La destruycion de la sagrada Troya:
Que navego por mar tan largo tiempo
Passando mill trabajos y fortunas. (77)

What Brenes Carrillo sees or chooses to see in this passage is the obvious, the excess, that is, the resemblance of the last line ("mill trabajos y fortunas") to the title of *Lazarillo*; he sees with Ricapito (1980, 100) that Lazaro is on a Homeric odyssey, or as he puts it: "The *Lazarillo* is an anti-*Ulysses*" ("*Lazarillo* es una anti-*Ulixea*," 58). But although he plunders the excess, Brenes Carrillo misses the essential point: Gonzalo Pérez expends energy translating *Ulixea* because it is, for him, a metaphor for the Jewish people. The destruction of sacred Troy in line 5 recalls the destructions of the temple in Jerusalem. In a much more tortured allusion, *Musa* in line 1 recalls Moses: the consonantal stem (*mss*) would be identical if the muses, plural, were invoked ("musas"); more important, the consonantal root (*ms*) is identical. Partly for these reasons, *Muça* is often transcribed as *Musa* to mean *Moses* in Arabic. To the converso mind the female vowel ending would be of little significance, and if gender had to be reconciled, it has been commonplace for centuries to conceive of

Moses mothering his children across the desert seas ("mar del de-
sierto"). For example, the twentieth-century Spanish writer Miguel
de Unamuno described one of his main characters in *San Manuel
Bueno, mártir* as a figure like Moses and Jesus, a "matriarchal man"
("aquel varón matriarcal"), a phrase that blind editors in Spain
changed, of course, to "patriarchal man" ("varón patriarcal," Unamuno
1979, 104), when Unamuno died before he could review the page
proofs to his masterpiece.

As I begin to suggest in the last chapter of this book, the great
seventeenth-century Spanish poet, Góngora, also begins his *Soledades* with the words *peregrino* and *musa*, knowing full well that
all Christian readers will understand the commonplace meanings of
"pilgrim" and "muse" and not see the references to Jews and Moses.
Christians are trained to think monoculturally; Jews have been forced
by their circumstances to think multiculturally; all people are capable
of, and do, in fact, practice, monocultural as well as multicultural
thought; all styles in all cultures at all times. But the experience of
each people also has its uniqueness.

Again, the secret opacity of *Lazarillo* is instructive: although
Brenes Carrillo cites on the same page (77) a passage from *Lazarillo*
with the word *pregonero* in it, he misses entirely that the words
peregrino (*pilgrim* or *wanderer*) in *Ulixea* (line 3) and *pregonero*
(*town crier*) in *Lazarillo* have an almost identical consonantal stem
pattern (*prgrn/prgnr*). In other words, the author of *Lazarillo* is interested in the text of *Ulixea* because Lazaro is a *pregonero peregrino*,
a wandering Jewish town crier whose job it is to confess/denounce
everybody's sin in public in the vernacular tongue ("declarar a bozes
sus delictos, pregonero hablando en buen romance," 173/71–72). A
Jew, accustomed from Hebrew to reading without vowels, is not likely
to miss the similarity in the consonantal stem pattern *prgrn/prgnr;*
Christian readers, accustomed to the presence of vowels, will easily
miss the point even when the texts are right in front of them. Even
the Christian reader who notices the similarity in sound between
peregrino and *pregonero* will not therefore make the assertion that
there is a similarity in meaning. In Hebrew and other Semitic languages, similar consonantal stem patterns denote like meaning, a
concept foreign to Romance languages.

Further, it is common knowledge that the Hebrew stem is often
understood both as a verb and as a noun, as the following passage
from a famous Hebrew grammar explains. This means that it would
have been normal for a person accustomed to the Hebrew language
to understand the stems of the words *peregrino* and *pregonero* (as

well as *confessó* and *confesso,* for example) both as verbs and as nouns with closely related meanings.

> Stems in Hebrew, as in the other Semitic languages, have this peculiarity, that by far the majority of them consist of three consonants. On these the meaning essentially depends, while the modifications of the idea are expressed rather by changes in the vowels. . . . Such a stem may be either a verb or a noun, and the language commonly exhibits both together, e.g., *zera he has sown, zara seed; hacham he was wise, hacham a wise man*. . . . The Jewish grammarians call the stem *shoresh root* . . . [but] the term *root*, as it is generally understood by linguists [as an irreducible biliteral unit], cannot be applied to the Semitic triliteral stem. . . . The law of the triliteral stem is so strictly observed in the formation of verbs and nouns in Hebrew (and in the Semitic languages generally), that the language has sometimes adopted artificial methods to preserve at least an appearance of triliteralism in monosyllabic stems. (Gesenius, 99–100)

The Hebrew mind will assume, therefore, that like consonantal stems have like meaning, and Jews, especially learned Jews, will automatically find a way to reconcile the semantic dissonance between words with similar consonantal stem patterns. This is precisely why Nebrija and Covarrubias seek a way to make *confesso* mean both Jew and confession: the consonantal stem *cnfss* is identical in both words, and therefore, to Nebrija and Covarrubias, the different meanings of the words must be reconciled. As the definition cited above shows, their reconciliation is based on the fact that the Hebrew root *jd* yields stems that mean *Jew* as a noun as well as *confess* as a verb.

With the concept *pregonero/peregrino, Lazarillo* confirms itself once more as a *confessó/confesso* text: the idea of confessing (more like slandering in public, as we shall soon see) is contained in *pregonero,* and the commonplace idea of the wandering Jew (*confesso*) is contained in *peregrino.* Of course, the Jews were forced to wander from persecution by the Spanish authorities, which is to say that, like Lazaro's father, the Jews of Spain "suffered persecution from justice," from the authorities (92/1).

Does this mean that Gonzalo Pérez is the author of *Lazarillo?* Maybe yes, maybe no. The answer to the inquisitorial question, like all such answers about the author of *Lazarillo,* will always remain permeable. Here is another part of the proof offered by Brenes Carrillo:

> Lazaro relates his life and whose child he was. Well, Your Grace should know before all things else that they call me Lazaro de Tormes,

son of Thomas Gonzales and of Antona Perez, natives of Tejares, a village in Salamanca. (1)

Cuenta Lazaro su vida, y cuyo hijo fue. Pues sepa V. M.[erced] ante todas cosas que a mi llaman Lazaro de Tormes, hijo de Thome goncales y de Antonia perez naturales de Tejares, aldea de Salamanca. (60)

From this text, Brenes Carrillo tortures the information that the first letter of the first word (*P*ues) plus the second letter of the second word (s*e*pa) plus the third letter of the third word (me*r*ced) plus the fourth letter of the fourth word (ant*e*) plus the fifth letter of the fifth word (toda*s*) come together to give the author of the book: P-E-R-E-S. What I mean by torture is not the fact that the critic looks for and finds a word puzzle in the text; it is legitimate and necessary to anticipate that there might be word puzzles in a converso text, as we well know from *Celestina*'s acrostic. Rather, I mean that if one merges intersubjectively with Brenes Carrillo's text and with other texts like his (I use his text only as an example here, and I do not mean to single him out, especially since my own 1980 article commits the same insensitivities to *Lazarillo*), one gets the distinct impression of the triumphant apprehension of a felon, almost as if one can hear the handcuffs snap together around the wrists behind the back of the author. In Brenes Carrillo's text, the handcuffs are the added bit of evidence that a document exists, dated 1542, certifying that Gonzalo Pérez, native of Segovia, legally recognized his illegitimate son, Antonio (Brenes Carrillo, 1987, 102–3).

But we have claimed that converso texts like *Lazarillo* will never yield their essence to inquisitorial critics, and, indeed, Brenes Carrillo comes away once more with excess from the text, not essence. First of all, Brenes Carrillo does not bother to ask why, if the name Perez is already in the text, the author takes the trouble to repeat it in a puzzle. Had he asked that question politely, the text might have revealed to him politely that in the fifth word *todas*, he needs the first *and* the fifth letters: the name is *Perets* in the puzzle, not *Peres*.

Christian readers see *Perez* clearly in the text; Jews who know how to look see the Hebrew name *Perets*, which means "breach," because one of the twins born in Genesis 38:29–30 makes an unnatural breach in the womb through which his brother is born first (which, by the way, is why in the prologue, Lazaro calls his work an unnaturally born trifle, like Lazaro himself; that is, a *nonada/nonata*). This means that when Brenes thinks, triumphantly, that he has found, in the 1542 document granting legal status to Antonio Pérez son of

Gonzalo Pérez, historical reference to the infamous love scandal—
the *caso*—in *Lazarillo*, the text sneers once more at the positivistic
handcuffs he has wrapped around it. The story in Genesis is a scandal
of mythological (not just historical) proportions, one which all Jews
contemplate year after year as the passage is read and explicated in
the synagogue. No time here for all its subtleties, except to note that
the biblical Perets, the *ur-Perets*, is the illegitimate son of Judah and
his daughter-in-law Tamar. In *Lazarillo* the point is that Perets is the
son of a Jew, or better, the children of all Jews, because Judah means
Jew literally, and Judah, therefore, son of Jacob and ancestor of David,
gave his name to all Jews. The biblical story also explains why the
Lazarillo passage revolves around the verb *tomar* and why Tormes
was chosen as the river of Lazaro's birth: the consonantal stem in
Tamar, the mother of Perets, and *tomar* are identical *(tmr)*, and the
consonantal stems in Tormes and Tamar are very similar *(trms/tmr)*.
What the historical document describes is raw material for artists
like the author of *Lazarillo*, not simply because there were scandals
at court at the time, but especially because those real-life scandals
had mythological import. Further, the story of Perets was of special
interest to Jewish and converso readers in Spain because it is alluded
to in the biblical book of Ruth, which is read in many synagogues on
Shabuoth. In Ruth 4:12–22, Perets is linked to the genealogical tree
of Jesse and David, and was therefore believed by Christians, including some New Christians, to be a direct ancestor of Jesus.

The names Gonzáles, Antona, and Pérez appear in *Lazarillo* not
simply because they refer to the author of the *Ulixea* who may have
had an illegitimate son named Antonio (we promised to accept all
claims made by Brenes Carrillo, but it is not beyond a reasonable
doubt that the Gonzalo Pérez of *Ulixea* and the certificate of legiti-
macy is the same person; note, for example, that the Gonzalo Pérez
with the bastard son was from Segovia, and that Brenes Carrillo
claims on page 85 that the author of *Ulixea* was from Aragon). These
names appear in *Lazarillo* especially because *Lazarillo* is a text about
inquisitions, and the same names also appear with frequency in the
records of the Spanish Inquisition. For example, Gutwirth (pp. 224,
233) cites two documents from Segovia; one concerns a Gonzalo Pérez
Jarada who appears as a witness explaining why he gave clothes to a
Segovian Jew. The other document cited by Gutwirth, dated 1490,
might one day be referred to by a positivist as a source for *Lazarillo*,
since in it Antón Pérez tells the Inquisition how at age ten or twelve
he went to live with Gonzalo del Río and his brother Rodríguez del
Río (this, to a positivist, would make the witness Antón Pérez del

Río, Anton Perez of the River, that is, Lazaro de Tormes, because Lazaro's mother's name was Antona Pérez).

It now seems clear that the choice of the names in *Lazarillo* is more artistic than historical. By using the names Antona, Gonzáles, and Pérez, the author has found a way to fill every artistic need of the work while making it impossible for the inquisitors to discover the artist if they found reason to do so. Gonzalo Pérez refers to the author of *Ulixea*—no doubt about it—but it cannot be made to refer indubitably to the author of *Lazarillo*. Artistically, to Christian humanist readers, the author of *Lazarillo* could be Gonzalez Pérez, translator of Homer; to Jewish readers the author of *Lazarillo* is the legendary Perets of the word game, son of Judah, father of Lazaro Gonzalez Pérez.

The strongest argument for Gonzalo Pérez as author of *Lazarillo* is the one that says that the author inserts herself (or himself; better, "that the writer is inserted") into the work in the same way that some other converso artists (like Diego de San Pedro, Fernando de Rojas, or Jorge de Montemayor) do, making artistic use of the literal, historical, and mythological significance of the author's real name. But we must consider also that if Jorge de Montemayor or Fernando de Rojas or even Diego de San Pedro (whose defense might be weakest: "Compúsolo San Pedro," "St. Peter composed it") were to have been threatened with the death penalty for their respective works, any good lawyer might have tried to set them free on the grounds that they had nothing to do with the works and were set up by enemies. The defense for Gonzalo Pérez (whose name is more common than, for example, Salman Rushdie), translator of Homer, might revolve around the strong possibility that some enemy of his has set him up, using his work and his domestic problems to get him killed; why would he, the defense would argue, make fun of himself and his dear (the prosecution would say bastard) son in print? Of course the prosecution would reply that any author can make similar claims; and, if the prosecuting lawyer and the Inquisition's legal consultants were learned conversos themselves, they would argue that Gonzalo Perets is proud of his illegitimate son and is trying to say to slanderers that he is like Judah, the father from whom the name of all Jews is derived, who was also tricked into having an illegitimate son. At which point the advocate for the defense would have panicked, and, to save a life and prolong the defense in the hope of a miracle that would stop all persecution of the Jewish people, he would have instructed his client to "confess" and point an accusing finger at some other Gonzalo Perets also capable of having written the work. And so on, ad infinitum, before any inquisitor who wanted to be fair, the accusing finger would point and, having wit, move on, barely surviving always at the very margin between life and death.

Pointing the finger at another Gonzalo Pérez is not simply to disclose oneself but also to speak artistically (much more than historically) for the author of *Ulixea*, for the witnesses named Gonzalo Pérez brought before the Spanish Inquisition, as well as for all the children of Perets, until some other final solution is devised to try, again, to wipe them all out from wandering the face of the earth. In other words, the author has fused in such intersubjective seamlessness with the material that the result is an experience that communicates, once again, the essence of converso verbal art, one major facet of which is to make authorship forever permeable and to a necessary extent irrelevant, except, of course, to prosecutors and other persecutors (the patterns are consonant) of the text. The anonymous act says powerfully, not as a mere topos of authorial modesty, but as a matter of life and death, "I give this work to my people; it is theirs; I have no need to (indeed I cannot in all honesty) appropriate it; the text speaks not for me but for itself." The reward for the artist is immortality, that is, the text itself with the author's *true* name and identity irresurrectibly buried under it, not unlike the man Lazaro buried under the text of *Lazarillo*. Resurrect the author if you can, kill the text! Condemn it, if you can, to what its prologue calls "the sepulchre of oblivion" ("la sepultura del olvido," 87/*xvii*).

As the pre-reader remembers the text of *Lazarillo*, it becomes amazing just how much might escape most readers, even though so much has already been plundered and exposed. Start with the name Lazaro de Tormes, for example. Is it patterned after popular novels of chivalry like Amadís de Gaula? Yes. Is it classical: Ulysses of Ithaca? Yes. Is it a style used by all cultures at all times: Gonzalo de Berceo, Jesus of Nazareth? Yes. Is it a typically converso name: Don Quixote de la Mancha, Pablo de Burgos, Gonzalo del Rio? Yes, especially del Rio.

Lazaro is de Tormes because he claims to have been born "inside the river Tormes" ("dentro del río Tormes"); that is, he is a little like Moses, not just like Amadís, the same Moses that Gonzalo Pérez saw consonantally in Homer's "Musa" (Brenes Carrillo, 77). But notice also that the assertion, "My birth took place in the river Tormes" ("Mi nascimiento fue dentro del río Tormes," 91/1) is repeated: "So that in truth I can call myself one born in the river" ("De manera que con verdad me puedo dezir nacido en el río," 92/1). To a converso mind, Moses is the archetypal converso who is confronted at some point in his life with the truth ("con verdad") about himself, and his circumcision and baptism are accomplished or annulled (depending on the type of converso) by the new Moses, *the* truth through Jesus; so that, on its mythological level, the old (testament) Mosaic text "in the river" ("dentro del rio") is glossed and made to reveal a new (testament) Christian text "in truth . . . born in the river" ("con verdad . . . nacido en el río"), which refers, again, on the mythological level (always leaving the literal peripheral level intact for the simple entertainment of those who do not delve—"no ahondaren"—into the centrally marginal sadness of the text), to baptism, forced, voluntary, or inherited, again depending on the type of converso; sadness, as reflected in the enigmatic sentence in the prologue "for *maybe* [I really do not see how, but one never knows, it just might be that] someone who read it might find *something* [I cannot, for the life of me, think what] that is pleasant to him ("*pues* podría *ser que* alguno, *que lo* lea, *halle* algo *que le* agrade") emphasis, and sincere public apology for my previous insensitive readings, mine.

But why Lazaro? The name Lazarus had acquired throughout the Middle Ages accretions of meaning in several linguistic fields. Does the text mean Lazarus the poor man of Luke 16 who could be carried up into the bosom of Abraham but who also could become like Dives and go to Hell? Yes, certainly. Lazarus, the man dead and buried for four days and resurrected by Jesus according to John 11? Yes, certainly. Lazarus, a blind man's guide? Yes, without a doubt, especially since the author is teaching blind critics ("those who do not delve deeply") how to read. Does the text mean Lazarus connected with words like *lazareto, lazarino,* and leprosy in Luke 16? Yes, definitely, and most essentially.

The best recent treatment I have read (since Malkiel 1952) of the relationship between Lazaro and leprosy is Manuel Ferrer-Chivite (1984, 375–79). Since Ferrer-Chivite's main focus on those pages is to show how Christians came to make Jews and conversos almost coterminous with leprosy, I should like to add to what he says only the perspective necessary for a converso text: that is, how Jews themselves considered leprosy. I have treated this topic at greater length elsewhere (Nepaulsingh 1989) and will present only a summary here.

For Jews, leprosy was a punishment for slander, the disease with which Miriam was punished for slandering Moses. The punishment was believed to be inflicted not only on the slanderer but also on those who listened to the slander; slander was seen as a contagion that spread like leprosy. So fearful were religious Jews of this disease that some rabbis recommended that it was very dangerous to praise

someone because the praise might elicit slander from a listening enemy of the person being praised, which would mean, of course, that
the person praising would immediately be contaminated by the disease. The effect was to make all observant Jews cultivate a clever
tongue and to despise those who tended to have a loose tongue when
speaking about other people.

In real life, all circumspect Jews would have avoided people like
Lazaro like the plague *whether or not he was speaking the truth*.
Observant Jews and some conversos would read *Lazarillo*, but only
as a simultaneously amusing and terrifying negative object lesson
against slander; they would have absolutely no doubt that Lazaro
was contaminating His Grace, and the tale would confirm their own
experience with the Spanish Inquisition as a despicably slanderous
and leprous institution.

The same text that was read by Christians as an entertaining collection of folktales well spiced with classical erudition and biblical
allusion would have been read by Jews and some conversos as a sad
and terrifying tragedy. *Lazarillo* means to tell its Christian readers
the story of a man who betters himself at considerable odds in a world
of hard knocks and makes it to some safe port however dubiously (89/
xviii); *Lazarillo* means to tell its Jewish and converso readers of a
man who tells a story that is funny only because the man is stupid
enough to think that funny slanderous stories can save him from the
Spanish Inquisition, an institution stricken with a fatally incurable
contagious disease. Some Jews and conversos might have read Lazaro
as a hero, as a kind of David conquering a Goliath with wily tricks,
as I will explain below; but most Jews will have read his narrative as
fatal to himself and to all those whom he indicts.

It is not essential to decide the reliability of Lazaro, or the veracity
of his story, as long as one understands the tradition in which he is
narrating. In this regard, Brenes Carrillo (1987) has done an inesti-
mable service to *Lazarillo* scholarship by riveting scrutiny on the
translation of the *Odyssey*, *Ulixea*, by Gonzalo Pérez. In a long article
of some forty-eight pages, Brenes Carrillo combs the *Ulixea* successfully for many reminiscences of *Lazarillo*. But Brenes Carrillo misses
a lot, and when he concludes that Gonzalo Peres is therefore the
author of *Lazarillo*, he fails to appreciate the extent to which all Jews,
and especially learned Jews, identified with Odysseus, and why.

It must be remembered, first of all, that, long before the birth of
Christianity, Jews, especially Alexandrian Jews, were used to reciting
and interpreting Homer in the original; so that Homer among Jews
is an ancient pre-Christian tradition. To demonstrate the depth to

which Jews, especially Spanish Jews, identified with Homer's *Odyssey* I will cite below key passages in the *Odyssey* (by no means all of them) that Brenes Carrillo omits in his long study but which no Spanish Jew who read or heard would ever forget.

When Odysseus, freed from Kalypso's island, swims ashore to the city of Scheria, he kneels before Arete, wife of Alkinoos, and entreats her to arrange for his return to his homeland, saying:

> Arete, daughter of Godlike Rhexenor, after much hardship
> I have come to your knees as a suppliant, and to your husband
> and to these feasters, on whom may the gods bestow prosperity
> in their own lives, and *grant to each to leave to his children*
> *his property in his house and the rights the people have given him.*
> But for me, urge that conveyance be given quickly
> to my country, since long now far from my people I suffer
> hardships
>
> (emphasis added, 115, VI:146–52)

Jews, who had suffered in Spain the loss of "property" and "house" as well as the legal "rights" the kings of Spain had given them, could not possibly read this passage and not remember it; no Jew in exile from Spain, or in Spain precariously, with relatives in exile, could fail to empathize with Odysseus' plea for a return to his homeland. And when Odysseus, in that same scene, assures Alkinoos that he is no god but mortal, saying, "Whoever it is of people you know who wear the greatest / burden of misery, such are the ones whom I would equal / for pain endured" (116, VI:211–13), most Jews, especially Spanish Jews, would identify themselves as the people who equal Odysseus in suffering. But if most Jews empathize with this Odysseus, they do not therefore sympathize with Lazaro: Lazaro does not compare well with the Odysseus who kneels before Arete and Alkinoos. Lazaro compares better with another Odysseus—Odysseus the liar.

Notice that I do not bother to cite the *Ulixea*. It is sufficient to know that the *Odyssey* was read and translated; it is not necessary to hunt sources in its translations. Specifically, I do not cite the *Ulixea* because it is a partial translation: it translates only the first thirteen books of the *Odyssey*. Since Brenes Carrillo is focusing on *Ulixea* and its translator, Gonzalo Pérez, he does not bother to ask why the translation stopped at Book XIII. It cannot be established beyond a reasonable doubt that Gonzalo Pérez or his publishers did not admire as much that part of the *Odyssey* after Book XIII, but it is more than curious that Book XIV of the *Odyssey* is where Odysseus begins to tell the *false* story of his life. In other words, *Lazarillo,* if it is, as it often sounds, a false account, seems to start where *Ulixea* left off. Lazaro, therefore can only be "un anti-Ulises" as Brenes Carrillo claims (p. 76) if one looks only at *Ulixea* and forgets about the rest of the *Odyssey.* If one looks at the rest of the *Odyssey,* it becomes crystal clear that Lazaro is narrating in the tradition of Odysseus.

Because it is in *Ulixea,* Brenes Carrillo cites (p. 78) the passage in Book IX:11–21 where Ulysses identifies himself truthfully as the son of Laertes. It would have been instructive if he had also cited the question to which Odysseus is responding, because it gives us additional insight on the much discussed omission of the reflexive in Lazaro's "a mí llaman Lázaro de Tormes" (one would normally hear in Spanish "a mí *me* llaman"). Alkinoos, suspicious of Odysseus' ability to deceive, asked him in Book VIII:547–52, 555:

> So do not longer keep hiding now with crafty purposes
> the truth of what I ask you. It is better to speak out.
> Tell me the name by which your mother and father called you
> in that place, and how the rest who live in the city about you
>   call you . . .
> Tell me your land, your neighbourhood and your city.

But this is not the only time in the *Odyssey* that Ulysses is asked to identify himself and tell his story. In Book XIV (185–87), the first of the final eleven mainly deceptive books that Gonzalo Pérez declined to translate, or failed to have published if he did translate, Eumaios, suspicious of Ulysses, asks him:

> But come now, aged sir, recite me the tale of your sorrows,
> and tell me this too, tell me truly, so that I may know it:
> What man are you and whence? Where is your city? Your parents?

In his reply to Eumaios, Ulysses confirms our claim that Lazaro narrates in the Homeric tradition by lying about his birth and by claiming that he is an illegitimate child (compare what follows with Lazaro's description of his parents):

> See, I will accurately answer all that you ask me.
>   . . .
> I announce that my origin is from Crete, a spacious
> land; I am son of a rich man, and there were many other
> sons who were born to him and reared in his palace. These were
> lawful sons by his wife, but a bought woman, a concubine,
> was my mother, yet I was favored with the legitimate
> sons by Kastor, Hylakos' son, whom I claim as father.
>
> (XIV:192, 199–204)

These echoes do not attribute authorship decisively to Gonzalo Pérez, although it would be silly to claim that he could not have written *Lazarillo* because his translation only went to Book XIII. The resemblances between the *Odyssey* and *Lazarillo* show, first of all, that the author of *Lazarillo* was clever enough to select material that would reflect classical mythology and Old and New Testament mythology, as well as folk legend, seamlessly into his masterpiece. Second, it is clear that *Lazarillo* can be convincingly perceived as a deceptive narrative written in the Homeric tradition of the last eleven books of the *Odyssey;* Gonzalo Pérez or some other clever writer decided to continue, in a different mode, where the *Ulixea* left off. Further, those who choose to guess how His Grace might have reacted to Lazaro's story might look for clues in the response of Eumaios:

> O sorrowful stranger, truly you troubled the spirit in me,
> by telling me all these details, how you suffered and wandered;
> yet I think some part is in no true order, and you will not persuade
>   me
> in your talk about Odysseus. Why should such a man as you are
> lie recklessly to me? But I myself know the whole truth.
>
> (XIV:361–65)

The main reason for quoting at such length from the *Odyssey* should not be to try to solve the question of authorship but to illustrate how Jews must have reacted to Homer's text in Spain from 1391 and after. Surely, Jews were aware that this was a pagan book, and there are many sections of the *Odyssey* that must have been repulsive to Jews, as, for example, when Eumaios, the swineherd, sleeps with the pigs at the end of Book XIV, or when Odysseus carves a loin of pork "edged with rich fat" and sends it as a choice gift to the singer Demodokos in VIII:474–81. But another passage of the *Odyssey* that would resound in the memory of Spanish Jews is the story Odysseus tells, even though it is false, about how some of his men fell into slavery in Egypt:

> On the fifth day we reached the abundant stream Aigyptos
> and I stayed my oarswept ships inside the Aigyptos river.
> Then I urged my eager companions to stay where they were, there
> close to the fleet, and to guard the ships, and was urgent with
>   them
> to send lookouts to the watching-places; but they, following
> their own impulse, and giving way to marauding violence,
> suddenly began plundering the Egyptians' beautiful

fields, and carried off the women and innocent children,
and killed the men, and soon the outcry came to the city.
They heard the shouting, and at the time when dawn shows, they
    came
on us, and all the plain was filled with horses and infantry
and the glare of bronze, and Zeus who delights in thunder flung
    down
a foul panic among my companions, and none was so hardy
as to stand and fight, for the evils stood in a circle around them.
There they killed many of us with the sharp bronze, *and others*
they led away alive, to work for them in forced labor;
but Zeus himself put this thought into my mind, as I will
tell you, but how I wish I had died and met my destiny
there in Egypt, for there was still more sorrow awaiting me.

(emphasis added, XIV:257–75)

In spite of the obvious differences, most Jews would remember a
story about someone suffering slavery, whether justified or not, in
Egypt, and compare it with the story of their own people; and most
Jews would remember, as they read Odysseus' wish that he should
have died in Egypt, how some of their ancestors complained to
Moses, when situations got bad in the desert wilderness, that they
wished he had left them to die in Egypt. Odysseus went on to say,
falsely, that he stayed seven years in Egypt before he could leave for
Phoenicia and Libya. The point, in my opinion, is therefore undeniable that Jews found in the *Odyssey* a text they could use to express
the despair they were feeling in Spain after 1391.

Although we attempt for convenience to establish that most Jews
would have reacted negatively to Lazaro's story, recognizing that it
was being told by Lazaro in the deceptive tradition of Odysseus, it
is important to remember that Jews and conversos were as varied a
group of human beings as any other group. Some Jews and conversos
surely would have seen Lazaro as a hero, also based on their knowledge of the *Odyssey*. Jewish and converso readers, as all readers of
the *Odyssey*, must have taken a terrible delight in the story at the end
of Book IX, where Odysseus, whom Polyphemos himself describes as
"a little man, niddering, feeble" (l. 515), blinds the fearsome giant in
his only eye. And Brenes Carrillo (pp. 80–85) compares that part of
the *Ulixea* with some sections in *Lazarillo*, especially when the blind
master's nose down his throat makes Lazaro vomit the sausage, and
when Lazaro sends the blind man crashing into the post. But reading
the episode about Polyphemos from the point of view of a certain
kind of Jew or converso, there is much, much more.

I assert that, for some Jews and conversos, Polyphemos with his one unnatural eye in the middle of his forehead and with his superior scorn for other people's gods was a perfect metaphor for the Spanish Inquisition. Some Jews who read the lines "The Cyclopes do not concern themselves over Zeus of the aegis, / nor any of the rest of the blessed gods, since we are far better than they" (ll. 275–77) might certainly think so; others would make the connection when Polyphemos orders Odysseus, "Tell me your name straightway / now" (ll. 355–56), and they would take delight when Odysseus replies, "Nobody is my name. My father and my mother call me / Nobody, as do all the others who are my companions" (ll. 366–67). All readers are revolted "when the Cyclopes had filled his enormous stomach, feeding / on human flesh" (ll. 296–97). But Jews would be particularly revolted that the Cyclopes swallowed flesh by "drinking down milk" (l. 297); and some Jews, at least, would have compared the Cyclopes' cooking human flesh over a fire with the Inquisition's burning at the stake; I have absolutely no doubt about it. To Jews who read this portion of the *Odyssey* as I suggest they might have, Lazaro becomes a wily heroic David who will trick the Inquisition just as Odysseus tricks and blinds the Cyclopes; and the blind man in the first *tratado* would have been, for these readers, as Brenes Carrillo claims (remaining blind to its Jewishness), a metaphor for Polyphemos. Other Jews and conversos would have pointed out, no doubt, that Lazaro does not reply like Odysseus that Nobody is his name; instead Lazaro names himself and many other people. Those who see Lazaro as a wily hero would then have replied that Lazaro was lying in the tradition of Odysseus.

Because converso texts conceal in order to save lives, it will probably be impossible for me to document, to the satisfaction of all readers, the assertion I make in the previous paragraph and in the title of this book, as well as the one I make later about Góngora's use of the episode of Polyphemos. Nevertheless, in making these assertions, I feel confident that there were many Spanish Jews and conversos, much cleverer than I, who would have made them after 1391; I am convinced that there are all styles of readers in all cultures at all times.

Anonymity in *Lazarillo* is enhanced when filtered through the *Odyssey*. Imagine the sheer and terrible delight the anonymous author of *Lazarillo* experienced as he ushered his little masterpiece into its inquisitorial environment, remembering *his Odyssey* and saying to the inquisitors who demand that he tell them his name, "Nobody is my name." But critics like Brenes Carrillo (again, I use him only as a metaphor for my own old ways of reading) would remind me that, as he slipped away joyfully from Polyphemos, Odysseus disclosed himself, saying:

> Cyclops, if any mortal man ever asks you who it was
> that inflicted upon your eye this shameful blinding,
> tell him that you were blinded by Odysseus, sacker of cities,
> Laertes is his father, and he makes his home in Ithaka.
>
> (IX:502–5)

By this, some inquisitorial readers would mean that the author of *Lazarillo* discloses himself as Gonzalo Pérez in the sentence, "Pues sepa Vuestra Merced ante todas cosas que a mi llaman Lazaro de Tormes, hijo de Tomé Gonzales y de Antona Pérez, naturales de Tejares, aldea de Salamanca." To which the anonymous author of *Lazarillo* could certainly reply, "That Gonzalo Pérez is not I. It is every Gonzalo Pérez that ever came before your Holy Inquisition. It is the Perets in the puzzle: it is all my people, who will one day blind your monocultural eye; it is every child of Perets who has ever suffered persecution from your justice."

Imagine, also, the terrible misgivings the anonymous author of *Lazarillo* (who could not possibly see, in the meaning of 1492, as far ahead as the significance of 1947 and of centennial years like 1992 when the edict of expulsion was rescinded) would have had as he read the curse of Polyphemos:

> Hear me, Poseidon who circle the earth, dark-haired. If truly
> I am your son, and you acknowledge yourself as my father,
> grant that Odysseus, sacker of cities, son of Laertes,
> who makes his home in Ithaka, *may never reach that home;*
> but if it is decided that he shall *see his own people,*
> and come home to his strong-founded house *and to his own
>   country,*
> let him come late, in bad case, with the loss of all his companions,
> in someone else's ship, *and find troubles in his household.*
>
> (emphasis added, IX:528–35)

For the Jew exiled from Spain, the curse of Polyphemos would have seemed a real and realizable threat to the promise of one day returning home to Israel. And even today, of course, ever since Jews have returned to a national home in 1947, there have been troubles in Israel's household. For the Jew or converso living in Spain around the time of the composition of the *Lazarillo*, the resonance of Homer's *Odyssey* would have been as strong as it had been for Jews for centuries, but the resemblance between Polyphemos and the Spanish Inquisition would have been inescapable. And the urge to write a book that would outwit the Inquisition, as Ulysses blinded Polyphemos, would have been irresistible for an artist capable of doing it as well as did the anonymous author of *Lazarillo*.

CHAPTER 5

Lazarillo as a *Confesso* Text

T HUS FAR, we have focused discussion mainly on the title of the work, *La vida de Lazarillo de Tormes y de sus fortunas y adversidades*. We have seen that Lazaro's life (*vida*) can be read as a true story patterned loosely after the lives of Christian saints, and, at the same time, it can be read as a completely false story after the tradition of Odysseus. In the meanings of the word *lázaro* we have found a strong association, among Jews, with slander and with leprosy. We have suggested that Jews would form a ridiculous comparison between the circumstances of Lazaro's birth in the river Tormes and the birth of Moses. And we have seen the fortunes and adversities of Lazaro's story designed to be ridiculously reminiscent of the fortunes and adversities of Odysseus. The justification for testing a reading of the work from a Jewish perspective was found in the contemporary meanings of the word *confesso*. Having found in one part of the text, the title, that Lazaro's narrative can be read within the tradition of Jewish slander and the tradition of the *Odyssey* known to Jews and conversos, we are now adequately prepared to examine the whole text more fully from the perspective of Jewish and converso readers. The text has normally been described from the point of view of Christians, and I will not repeat those entirely valid readings here, except when necessary for contrast.

Reading the work from the perspective of Jews and conversos, one finds that the theme *confessó/confesso* is maintained throughout the work, in the prologue as well as in all seven *tratados*. In the prologue, Lazaro confesses that he is no more of a saint than his neighbors (89/ *xviii*), an admission that can be made to refer negatively to the neighbor who might most interest His Grace, the Archpriest of San Salvador who made Lazaro and his wife rent a house next to his (175/72).

In the first *tratado*, Lazaro's father is not the only person who confesses; Lazaro's own confession helps convict his mother and her black lover (94/3). The first *tratado* is also Lazaro's confession of his lineage ("cuyo hijo fue," 91/1). Lazaro confesses that his biological parents have names (Gonzales, Pérez) that appear with some frequency in the records of the Inquisition (91/1), and that the man he refers to as his "stepfather" (*padrastro*, 93/2, 94/3) is a black Moorish stableboy. In spite of these admissions, Lazaro makes (what would appear to any converso who was forced to know the New Testament) ridiculous attempts to prove that his lineage is impeccably Christian.

In the eyes of a converso reader, Lazaro's claim that his blind master took him not as a mere manservant but as a son ("no por mozo sino por hijo," 95/4) is a transparently false attempt to counterfeit a Christian heritage. Among his experiences as this blind man's son, Lazaro selects to confess to seven that best attest to his Christian education. The episode on the road out of Salamanca with the stone bull is Lazaro's conversion on the road to Damascus: "I awoke from the simpleness in which, as a child, I was sleeping" ("desperté de la simpleza en que, como niño, dormido estaba," 96/5) is a reference to I Corinthians 13:11 "When I was a child").

Lazaro's stealing bread from the blind man's bag is meant to link him to Christianity in two ridiculous ways—first, the verb used euphemistically for stealing is *sangrar* ("to bleed" or "to drain by bleeding," 98/8), which is intended to recall the "bleedings" of the flour sacks (92/1) for which Lazaro hopes his father went to Heaven (92/1); and second, Lazaro's vital attachment to bread for life is intended to recall the fact that Jesus proclaimed himself to be "the bread of life" in John 6. (This allusion would have been very important to conversos, as we will soon see in the discussion of the second *tratado*.)

The episode with the coins (*blancas*), in which Lazaro changes coins for lesser value, is meant to recall the disdainful (later to become characteristically anti-Jewish) virulence with which Jesus treated the money changers outside the temple (Matthew 21:12).

When Lazaro says that the blind man assured him that because of all his experiences with wine, wine was his true father ("eres en más cargo al vino que a tu padre," 110/16–17), the ridiculous claim to Christian heritage is the fact that Jesus proclaimed himself to be the true vine (John 15:1), which would make Lazaro a spiritual "son" of Jesus Christ.

The discreet accounting lesson (106/13) that Lazaro says he

learned in the episode with the bunch of grapes is meant to recall, in a way only a stranger to Christianity would claim, the miracle of the five loaves and five fishes that Jesus shared among the multitude of over five thousand people (Matthew 14); the ridiculous connection is that the blind man shared the grapes and miraculously saw how many Lazaro was eating at a time.

The episode of the sausage that Lazaro is forced to vomit and return to its owner is a ridiculous reference to the admonition of Jesus, "Render unto Caesar the things that are Caesar's" (Mark 12:17).

And the final episode, in which Lazaro says he prevented the blind man from crossing over to the other side of the river, is meant to recall the Christian imagery of crossing the river Jordan to get from one side of life to the other side, that is, to Heaven. In this last episode with the blind man, it can be said that here Lazaro is born or reborn; here the child Lazarillo becomes, prematurely, a man, referring once more to Lazaro's claim that he was truly born in a river.

This final reference to baptism or rebirth implied in the "successful" crossing over to the other side would be interpreted by a converso not merely as an awkward pretense at crossing over from Judaism to Christianity, but especially as a feigned acceptance of Christian confession, since the river Jordan was clearly associated with baptism *and* confession: "Then went out to him Jerusalem and all Judea and all the region about the Jordan, and they were baptized by him in the river Jordan, confessing their sins" (Matthew 3:5, 6).

Thus we see that, although the first *tratado* might be interpreted by Christian readers as a series of folk stories that poke gently mocking and adoring fun at Christianity, to a converso reader the same *tratado* represents the ridiculous claims of a converso to Christian heritage through upbringing, indoctrination, baptism, and confession. Confession is an act that Jews perform formulaically, as on Yom Kippur, when a Jew confesses all sins generically without entering into any details, presumably since God has no need of the details. Lazaro is obviously not practiced in the sacrament of Christian confession; when called upon to confess, he assumes that he will be pardoned if he simply gives the impression of telling all. However, his expansive and detailed confession in the first *tratado*, meant to prove his true Christian upbringing, betrays, instead, his real non-Christian nature.

Most Jewish and converso readers would have been reminded by Lazaro's confession of the kind of confessions recorded by the Spanish Inquisition during the thirty- or forty-day period of grace granted whenever a tribunal was set up. Lea described those confessions in the following way:

The confessions under Edicts of Grace are pitiful reading. The poor creatures naturally admit as little as possible, in the hope of diminishing the pecuniary penance. They strive to extenuate their errors and throw the blame on those who misled them; they grovel before the inquisitors, profess the deepest contrition and promise strenuous perseverance in the faith. They rarely go out of their way to compromise others, but they frankly state who it was that perverted them and have no hesitation in implicating parents and kindred and benefactors. Unlike the priest in the confessional, the inquisitors abstained from interrogating them or seeking information about themselves or others. It was not their policy to stimulate confession and the penitent was allowed to state as much or as little as he chose. The results are evidently the unassisted work of the penitents, inconsistent, rambling, frequently almost unintelligible, whether written by themselves or taken down verbatim by the notaries, for it was essential that they should be of record, to be brought up against them, in the probable case of backsliding or of testimony to omitted facts.
    (Lea 1906, II, 459; see also I, 165–66)

The resemblances to Lazaro's story are obvious: the penitents admitted little; extenuated their errors; cast blame elsewhere; implicated parents, relatives, and benefactors; pretended Christian piety; opted to tell as much or as little as they chose; wrote down confessions unassisted; rambled inconsistently and unintelligibly at times; and, above all, through their incomplete testimony left themselves legally vulnerable when a full accounting was requested. Even though there are also obvious dissimilarities, it is feasible to assert that Lazaro's confession is reminiscent of the confessions made to the Spanish Inquisition under edicts of grace in exchange for reduced sentences.

In Lazaro's confession of his Christian heritage as learned from the blind man, none of the references to the New Testament forms a clear and unequivocal parallel with what is happening to Lazaro; that kind of clarity would have been risky. That the New Testament is being alluded to is clear, but the allusion never quite matches the context. For example, having one's head pounded into a stone bull is not really comparable to being blinded by a divine light for three days, as is explained in the book of Acts 9:1–9. The reference is not to Acts, yet the text makes it clear that it is referring to Paul by comparing the naïveté of one who thinks like a child to the enlightenment of one who has had an illuminating experience; it evokes Paul's famous letter (about the power of love) to the church at Corinth, specifically to his dictum *cum essem parvulus*.

The author of *Lazarillo* creates an atmosphere of sanctity with a well-known pious reference that diverts attention from the cruelty of what is happening. The Christian reader is so familiar with the phrase "when I was a child" that the connection is not made between having one's head cruelly pounded into a stone bull and the lesson from Saint Paul about the power of love. The Christian reader is also diverted from seeing that this represents Lazaro's conversion to Christianity, but the converso reader is encouraged to think about conversion because any reference to Paul sparks the thought of conversion in the mind of Jews and conversos.

What is clear to the Jewish and converso reader is seen opaquely, as through a glass darkly, by the Christian reader; it might not be an accident that Paul's reference to seeing through a glass darkly is also found in the same context (I Corinthians 13:12) and in the very next verse after the reference to "when I was a child." The indirectness, the references *al sesgo* (on a tangent) are deliberately designed to blind the superficial inquisitorial reader and simultaneously to enlighten the oppressed minority of readers who know how to ferret out the deeper meanings of the text (as we shall see later in *La Diana*, Jorge de Montemayor explains in some detail this technique of diverting attention from the coded message). An analysis like this one of the stone bull could be made for all seven of Lazaro's experiences with the blind man to show that they constantly attract and divert attention, with the primary purpose of blinding the inquisitorial reader; but much remains to be said about the other *tratados*.

By a curious coincidence, the action in the second *tratado* takes place in a town outside of Toledo called Maqueda. Editors have noted that the town's name is probably of Jewish origin, after the the biblical "Magda" (113/20), leaving the impression that it was, at some point in its history, a Jewish town. But there is more. In 1467, the canons of Toledo farmed out to a Jew the collection of taxes from the sale of bread made at Maqueda. An official of the town of Maqueda beat the Jew and confiscated the bread; the dispute flared up and led eventually to the hanging of two converso leaders (Lea 1906, I, 127–28). It would not be surprising if conversos, reading the emphasis on bread and beating in the text of *Lazarillo*, understood a reference to the bread riots at Maqueda in 1467.

The theme *confessó/confesso* is carefully and artistically continued in the second *tratado*. Here Lazaro confesses by denouncing himself more literally than in the first *tratado:* the key he has hidden in his mouth betrays him as he sleeps and snores. This clue would not be missed by the Jewish and converso reader—thinking that he is saving himself from harm, Lazaro exposes himself to cruel punishment; he is beaten like a treacherous serpent and expelled from his breadly paradise; so much for the confession part of the *confessó/confesso*

theme. As far as Jews and conversos were concerned, this reference
to a breadly paradise ("paraíso panal" 119/25) is crucial, especially
since the author is careful to put its evangelical source on the same
page and in the mouth of Lazaro himself: "I used to dissemble, and
in my secret prayer and devotions and supplications, I used to say,
'Saint John and blind him'" ("Yo disimulaba, y en mi secreta oración
y devociones y plegarias, decía: Sant Juan y ciégale," 119/25). This is
a reference, for those who know, to John 6; it is not accidental that
the expressions "dissemble," "secret prayer," and "blind him" are used
in this passage because they refer not simply to what Lazaro says he
is doing here to his investigating master, but also, obliquely, to what
many conversos, like Lazaro, were forced to do: pretend, pray in
secret, and blind the Inquisition.

The sixth chapter of John is not just the place where the miracle
of the five loaves and five fishes is recounted and the place where
Jesus identifies himself as the bread of life, but most important, for
the Jewish and converso reader, it is the place where Jesus invites
conversion from the law of Moses; it is, therefore, the locus classicus
for divisiveness between Jews and conversos:

> Jesus then said to them, "Truly, truly, I say to you, it was not Moses
> who gave you the bread from heaven; my Father gives you the true
> bread from heaven. . . ." They said to him, "Lord, give us this bread
> always." Jesus said to them, "I am the bread of life; he who comes to
> me shall not hunger. . . ." The Jews then murmured at him, because
> he said, "I am the bread which came down from heaven." They said,
> "Is this not Jesus, the son of Joseph, whose father and mother we
> know? How does he now say, 'I have come down from heaven'?" Jesus
> answered them, "Do not murmur among yourselves. . . . I am the
> bread of life. Your fathers ate the manna in the wilderness, and they
> died. This is the bread which comes down from heaven, that a man
> may eat of it and never die. I am the living bread which came down
> from heaven. . . ." (John 6:32–51)

When Lazaro equates bread with life and death throughout the second *tratado*, and especially when the text refers to "Sant Juan," the
converso or Jewish reader who knows the New Testament and the
words attributed to Jesus about converting from the law of Moses to
the law of Jesus cannot possibly miss what must have been a context
for painful debate among Jews and conversos, particularly in Spain
from 1391 onward, but as it was also at the time of Jesus.

The third *tratado* is probably the one in which the Jewish and
converso reader would find most evidence of the *confessó/confesso*
theme. First of all, Lazaro literally confesses once more when the

authorities demand that he disclose what he knows of his master, the squire: "I promised to say what they were asking me" ("prometile de decir lo que me preguntaban," 154/59); in this *tratado* also, the squire himself confesses his life and circumstances to Lazaro (147/54). So much for the confession part of the theme. As far as the Jewish and converso perspective is concerned, many critics have suspected that the squire is converso, and that Lazaro has more sympathy for the squire than for any of his other masters ("those people it is fair to dislike," says Lazaro comparing other people to the squire, "and have pity on this man," "aquellos es justo desamar, y aqueste de haber mancilla," 142/49).

Lazaro's use of the word *mancilla*, which Covarrubias defines as the diminutive of *mancha*, meaning "stain," would not have escaped the eyes of converso and Jewish readers, who would understand not just "pity" but especially "stain on one's lineage," as in the expression cited in the *Diccionario de Autoridades* "it is not the stain of a Jew" ("no es mancha de judío"). Critics have also pointed to many subtle ways in which the text seeks to identify Lazaro with the squire, and rather than repeat these here, I should like to emphasize instead, in a manner not done before, as far as I know, the principal way in which the squire and Lazaro identify themselves as conversos in the eyes of Jewish and converso readers.

The squire is clearly a social climber: his biggest goal in life seems to be to work for a gentleman of high social standing, "un señor de título" (151/56); this is also Lazaro's life ambition: to get close to, to cosy up to, the right people ("arrimarse a los buenos," 92/2, 175/73). A long-standing belief among Jews is that one of the three principal causes of apostasy is social climbing. Even before the birth of Christ, the Jewish philosopher Philo described clearly three kinds of apostates from Judaism: those who yield to the weakness of the flesh and break the laws of diet and marriage; those who are intellectually uprooted because they think that the knowledge they have acquired, from philosophy, for example, is more sophisticated than the laws of Judaism; and those who seek to better their material position and seek wealth by cultivating social connections. The following passage from Philo's *Life of Moses* leaves no doubt that Jews would recognize both Lazaro and his master, the squire, as apostates and conversos from Judaism:

> Men in general, even if the slightest breeze of prosperity does only blow their way for a moment, become puffed up and give themselves great airs, becoming insolent to all those who are in a lower condition

than themselves, and calling them dregs of the earth, and annoyances, and sources of trouble, and burdens of the earth, and all sorts of names of that kind, as if they themselves had the permanence of their prosperity securely sealed in their possession, though even the morrow may find them no longer where they are. For nothing is more unstable than Fortune, who moves human affairs up and down on the draughtboard of life, and in a single day pulls down the lofty and exalts the lowly on high; and though they see and know full well that this is always happening, they nevertheless look down upon their relations and friends and transgress the laws under which they were born and bred, and subvert the ancestral customs to which no blame can justly attach, by adopting different modes of life, and in their contentment with the present, lose all memory of the past.
(Philo 1950, 291, 293; Wolfson 1968, 77–78)

Social climbing is common to all cultures, and thus not a typically Jewish trait, and Lazaro makes the squire say that what he describes is typical behavior in the palaces of the nobility at that time (152/57), but these facts lend perfect cover to the converso code by diverting attention away from Judaism and toward common practice. They do not change the fact that Jewish and converso readers would have seen the squire and Lazaro for what they know them to be: not just social climbers of the common human sort, but especially social-climbing Jewish apostates.

To Jewish and converso readers, the squire reveals himself in much less subtle ways than his characteristic apostasy. For example, when the squire talks about converting oneself from man to trump card ("porque de hombre os habéis de convertir en malilla," 150–51/56), this is no simple reference to a card game, but a perfect description of the type of person Lazaro and the squire aspire to be. The *Diccionario de Autoridades* defines *malilla* as a "person of ill intentions, who with gossip and tales does evil to others, and in order to ingratiate himself does them in" ("sugeto de mala intención, que con chismes y cuentos hace mal a los otros, y por congraciarse los desaviene"). This is precisely what Lazaro, in the eyes of Jewish and converso readers, is doing, and precisely what the squire says he would do if he landed a job with the right master: he would be a "malicioso mofador," he would "malsinar" and "pesquisar y procurar de saber vidas ajenas para contárselas" (151/57).

Whatever these words describe to non-Jewish readers, they had very specific meanings to Jewish and converso readers. In their religious contexts *malicioso* refers to slander, and *mofador* refers to those who scoff at religion (the *Diccionario de Autoridades* gives these examples—"dexó de ser calumniado de la malicia" and "gran mofador de las cosas de la religión"). *Malsinar* is a verb, believed to be of Hebrew derivation, which refers specifically, among Jews, to the act of denunciation of Jews against each other before the Spanish Inquisition. *Pesquisar* ("investigating" or, better, "spying") and finding out information about other people's lives in order to inform the authorities also refer clearly, at least from the perspective of the Jewish and converso reader, to the proceedings of the Spanish Inquisition.

Most important, the squire reveals that he would compose a kind of converso text: he says clearly that he would tell his master things that would appear on the surface to be to the benefit of co-workers but that would result in their harm: "If he was quarrelling with a servant of his, [I would] add a few sharp jibes to inflame his rage, and [in such a way] that it might seem to be in favor of the guilty [servant]" ("Si riñese con algún su criado, dar unos puntillos agudos para le encender la ira, y que paresciesen en favor de el culpado," 151/57). This, by the way, is one reason that the rabbis admonished against praising people in public, because praise, in the presence of an adversary of the person being praised, leads to and becomes coterminous with slander.

The brief fourth *tratado* has been shown by several critics to contain Lazaro's denunciation of the sexual inclinations of the Mercedarian friar. To what has been said (by Abrams, Sieber, and Walsh and Thompson) about the link between shoes and sexual activity, I add only the example in number 64 of Alfonso el Sabio's *Cantigas de Santa María*, "How the woman whose husband left her entrusted to the charge of Saint Mary could not put on her foot nor take off the shoe a lover gave to her" ("Como la mujer cuyo marido le dejó encomendada a Santa María no pudo meter en el pie ni descalzar el zapato que un amante le dió"). Jews and conversos would, like some Christians, recognize the allusion to homosexuality in Lazaro's words, "and for other things which I do not speak" ("y por otras cosas que no digo," 157/61), because homosexuality was widely known as the *unspeakable* sin (Sieber 1978, 58 n26). The reaction among Jews to Lazaro's relationship with a homosexual, however that relationship may have been perceived, would have been much more severe than the reaction of Christian readers.

Among Jews, the punishment for homosexuality was death by stoning, which is one of the reasons that homosexuality among Jews was considered rare. The rabbis did not think that Jews were less susceptible to homosexuality than others, but they tended to attribute homosexuality to the kind of trap that social-climber Jews fell into because of their desire to assimilate with non-Jews, and they referred to a period in Jewish history when there were male sacred prostitutes in the Temple in Jerusalem:

> Sodomy was sometimes part of the heathen worship, with male sacred prostitutes known to the Hebrews as kedeshim (s. *kadesh*), ministering sexually to the worshippers; and the Hebrews who refused to accept immorality in secular form succumbed to it more readily when draped in religious garb. Thus sacred sodomy, alien and hateful to the ancient Hebrew cult, penetrated into Judea at the time of the early kings from the idolatry of the Canaanites. Under Rehoboam, and probably due to the influence of his mother, idolatry became rampant in Judea "and also sodomites were in the land" (I Kings 14:24). His grandson Asa tried to cleanse the Temple in Jerusalem of that practice; a further attempt was made by his great-grandson Jehoshaphat; but sodomy in the Temple was not eradicated until the vigorous reforms of the righteous king Josiah. . . . The [later] Levitical law went the whole way and was evidently quite effective in eradicating sodomy among the Jewish people. (Epstein 1967, 135,36)

Most Jewish readers would have attributed Lazaro's association with homosexuality to his social climbing, and learned Jewish readers would have seen him as a ridiculous *kadesh,* a sacred prostitute like those of the Temple in the time of the early kings; his wife would be viewed as the Archpriest's *kedeshah,* or female prostitute. Jewish laws about forbidden intercourse were common knowledge, and commentators like Maimonides devoted much attention to the topic.

In the fifth *tratado,* confession continues to mean denunciation and to refer specifically to Jews. The law officer (*alguazil*) pretends to denounce the pardoner (*buldero*) whom he serves; the officer is in turn denounced by the pardoner and made to confess that he was an agent of the devil (165/68–69). Lazaro then confesses that he was taken in at first but denounces both the pardoner and his assistant, the law officer: "I confess my sin that I too was frightened by it . . . but . . . I came to realize how I had been deliberately set up by my industrious and inventive master" ("Confieso mi pecado que también fui dello espantado . . . mas . . . conoscí como había sido industriado por el industrioso y inventivo de mi amo," 165/69). But the text also lets the careful reader see the strong resemblance among Lazaro and the law officer and the pardoner. Like the pardoner, Lazaro has confessed to being capable of "very subtle inventions" ("muy sotiles invenciones," 158/62) and "clever malicious artifices" ("mañosos artificios," 159/63) and, especially, to have the same kind of "extremely loose tongue" ("desenvoltísima lengua," 159/62) that he attributes to the pardoner, the kind of slanderous tongue rabbis warned against.

The meaning of all this to the Jewish reader is made very clear because, as Claudio Guillén has noted (1966, 168 n376), the phraseology used by the pardoner in the sham pardoning of the law officer is similar to the words used by officers of the Spanish Inquisition during the sentencing of a converso for Judaizing: "Praying to Our Lord, for I was not seeking the death of the sinner, but his life and repentance" ("Suplicando a Nuestro Señor, pues no quería la muerte del pecador, sino su vida y arrrepentimiento," 164/68). In other words, to the Jewish and converso reader, the pardoner pardons on the same textual biblical authority, and by implication, therefore, on the same fabricated testimony, as the Holy Spanish Inquisition.

In the sixth *tratado*, the brief one-sentence reference to Lazaro's service with the tambourine painter would, in the eyes of Jewish and converso readers, confirm Lazaro's commitment to social climbing because of the proverbs, "He who has money paints [his or her] tambourines [or has them painted]" ("Quien tiene dineros pinta panderos"), and "The tambourine will be [painted] according to the money [paid for it] ("segun sea el dinero será el pandero"); social climbing, as we have noted, is the mark of the Jewish apostate. Lazaro's acquisition of clothes and sword, so reminiscent of the squire in the third *tratado*, would also confirm Lazaro's social-climbing converso status, from the perspective of Jews and conversos.

In this *tratado* Lazaro also deliberately denounces his master the chaplain as a converso who would not work or accept the proceeds of work done on Saturdays: "I used to give every day to my master thirty earned maravedis, and on Saturdays I earned for myself and all the rest during the week, at thirty maravedis" ("Daba cada día a mi amo treinta maravedís ganados, y los sábados ganaba para mí, y todo lo demás, entre semana, de treinta maravedís," 171/70). Christian readers would probably notice that, depending on the punctuation of the sentence, Lazaro had begun, for the first time, to earn as much as the person he was working for; Jewish and converso readers, however, sensitive to the accusation that one of them had betrayed Jesus for thirty pieces of silver, would not fail to notice, also, the repetition of the number thirty pieces of money in the same sentence.

In the seventh *tratado*, Lazaro first serves as an assistant—"man of justice" ("hombre de justicia," 172/71)—to an officer of the law, but he leaves it because he experiences it as a dangerous job ("oficio peligroso") when he and his master are chased with stones and sticks by persons who had sought refuge for their alleged crimes in the bosom of the church ("unos retraídos," 172/71). To most Christian readers, *retraídos* would probably not refer specifically to any particular group but to anyone who sought refuge in a church; to Jews and conversos, however, seeking refuge in the bosom of the church in anticipation of, and often in a desperate effort to deter, being accused of crimes they may or may not have committed, was an obvious and commonly used strategy to avoid persecution. Indeed, the *Diccionario de Autoridades*, in its definition of "retrahimiento," cites a passage from Fonseca that supports this interpretation of *retraídos:* "Ezekiel was in Babylon, and God brought him to Jerusalem so that he could see the secret abominations the most elderly were committing, every one of them in the utmost secrecy of their place of refuge" ("Ezechiel estaba en Babilonia, y trúxole Dios a Jerusalén, para que viesse las abominaciones secretas que hacían los más ancianos, cada uno en lo más secreto de su *retrahimiento*"). Conversos were accused of committing secret abominations in private.

In the rest of the seventh *tratado*, of course, Lazaro achieves the highest point of his career when he gets a job as a *pregonero;* in other words, he gets to do officially what we have seen him do in each of the previous six *tratados*, denounce other people's wrongdoings (and his own) in public (173/72). Lazaro's description of his current circumstances implicates his master, the Archpriest, because he admits that the Archpriest is aware of what people are thinking and still persists in maintaining the arrangement rather than avoid suspicion. Lazaro also confirms that he has evidence that his wife bore three children before he married her: "And on more than three occasions they even proved to me that before she married me she had given birth three times" ("y aún por más de tres veces me han certificado que antes que comigo casase había parido tres veces," 175–76/73).

There can be no doubt, therefore, that the theme *confessó/confesso*—that a converso is by dictionary definition a Jew who characteristically confesses as if to the Inquisition—pervades the entire text of *Lazarillo* and is found in every *tratado*. To Jewish and converso readers, Lazaro is not merely an exemplary Christian hammered to perfection in the school of hard knocks. To Jewish and converso readers, Lazaro is above all else a *confesso*, as dictionaries approved by the Spanish Inquisition define that term; his constant confessions throughout his narrative, and the confessionary nature of the narrative itself, betray him as a *confesso*, a Jew, like the character in *Pícara Justina* (cited in one dictionary) who confessed so much that they called her a *confessa*, another word for conversa or Jewess. In this important sense, therefore, Lazaro's narrative is a converso text that is recognizable by Christians and by Jews in contrary ways.

It is also apparent that the environment of the text is inquisitorial. For many readers, especially for Christian readers, this inquisitorial environment is harmless and quotidian; García de la Concha, for example, cites Andres Navaggero, who visited Toledo in 1525, to the effect that nobody paid much attention to the fact that clergymen had concubines:

> Andres Navaggero visited the imperial city in 1525 and he testifies in his *Journey Through Spain* that "the owners of Toledo, and of the women in particular, are the clergymen, who have beautiful houses and spend and celebrate giving themselves the best life in the world, without reprimand from anyone." It seems that the testimony coincides in its presentation, and even in its verbal tone, with the *Lazarillo*. But it is fitting not to rush to conclusions. In fact, the Inquisition does not alter and leaves the seventh *tratado* substantially intact. The contemporaries devour the book and split their sides with laughter. Attention was centered, preferably, on preventing the concubines from living under the same roof or the children of adultery from holding posts in the same parish.

> Andres Navaggero visitó la ciudad imperial en 1525 y testifica en su *Viaje por Espana* que "los amos de Toledo, y de las mujeres precipue, son los clérigos, que tienen hermosas casas y gastan y triumphan dándose la mejor vida del mundo, sin que nadie les reprenda." Parece que el testimonio coincide en su planteamiento, y hasta en su tono verbal, con el *Lazarillo*. Pero conviene no precipitarse. De hecho, la Inquisición no se inmuta y deja sustancialmente intacto el Tratado VII. Los coetáneos devoran el libro y se desternillan de risa. . . . La atención se centra, preferente, en evitar que las barraganas vivan bajo el mismo techo o que los hijos adulterinos sean empleados en oficios de la misma parroquia. (1972, 247)

Doubtless, for some Christian readers, the contents of the *Lazarillo* would be a laughing matter, and the scandal a common occurrence; indeed, Lazaro himself is made to listen to the laughter of others while he cries because of the cruelty inflicted upon him (109/16, 128/35). But for Jewish and converso readers, what is a laughing matter for Christians is part of a cruel and painful inquisitorial environment.

It is no laughing matter that, whether Lazaro's story is true or not, people like Lazaro's father were imprisoned, punished, and sent to the front lines to be killed, that Lazaro's mother received the *usual* hundred lashes with the whip and that her black lover was whipped and scalded with hot oil, presumably to whiten his skin and make him look leprous. To the Jewish and converso reader, the violence and threats that pervade the text of *Lazarillo* are as real as the massacre of 1391 and after, during which Christians beat Jews and conversos mercilessly and threatened them into conversion. In the first *tratado,* the authorities threaten the child Lazarillo and force him to confess through fear (94/3); Lazaro's first two masters beat him mercilessly; in the third *tratado,* the authorities threaten Lazaro into confession (154/58); in the fifth *tratado,* the pardoner and his peace officer fake a fight to the death which all the neighbors present have reason to believe to be real (160/63); and in the seventh *tratado,* Lazaro's master is attacked with sticks and stones by those who had taken refuge in a church, and Lazaro himself flees from the violence and from the physically dangerous job; in the seventh *tratado,* as well, it should not go unnoticed that Lazaro has threatened to kill himself fighting anyone who accuses his wife of wrongdoing. Those who insist that Lazaro's narrative must be believed and that his fortune is at its height should also believe that this is a real threat to everyone, including His Grace, especially since Lazaro swears solemnly that he will fulfill it: "Because I will swear on the consecrated Host, that she is as good a woman as any that lives within the gates of Toledo. Whoever tells me anything else, I will kill myself with him" ("Que yo juraré sobre la hostia consagrada, que es tan buena mujer como vive dentro de las puertas de Toledo. Quien otra cosa me dijere, yo me mataré con él," 176–77/74)

Besides, to return to García Concha's dismissal of the scandal as something the Spanish Inquisition would have ignored, not all readers of *Lazarillo* would have agreed that the scandal (*caso*) Lazaro is asked to explain in full is about clerical concubines. Some Jewish and converso readers would have noticed that Lazaro says, in talking about his job as wine seller, "Almost all the things having to do with the office (*oficio*) pass through my hands" ("Casi todas las cosas al oficio tocantes pasan por mi mano," 173/72). Taking into consideration that a key technique for deception in a coded converso text was the incrustation of the code in a different, though not altogether distant, context, some Jewish and converso readers would understand Lazaro to be saying that almost all the business of the *Holy Office,* that is, of the Spanish Inquisition in that district, passed through his hands. This would not have been a far-fetched interpretation, because one of the dictionary definitions of the word *oficio* at that time, according to the authoritative *Diccionario de Autoridades,* was: "Holy Office: the name by antonomasia for the Tribunal of the Inquisition" ("Santo *oficio.* Se llama por antonomasia el Tribunal de la Inquisición"). This would mean that Lazaro's employer, the Archpriest of San Salvador, might be an employee of the Spanish Inquisition, a commissioner perhaps. Commissioners and other officials of the Inquisition were

not permitted to employ their relatives or servants in the work of the
Spanish Inquisition (Lea 1906, II, 219), which implies that relatives
and servants were hired, necessitating the rule. Conversos especially
were strictly prohibited from working for the Inquisition, and all
applicants were required to verify their lineage before they could be
employed by the Holy Office. Vuestra Merced, "Your Grace," might
be an inquisitor who has written asking Lazaro to make a full confession about his employment by the Archpriest, or about some other
case that has been brought to his attention. Lazaro chooses to tell a
diversionary story about his life, and, finally, about concubinage. The
point is that concubinage might just be one minor part of the scandal
to which the text refers.

It could be argued that the violence the text describes repeatedly
is meted out for good cause to those who deserve it. But here again,
from the perspective of a Jewish or converso reader, the text makes
it quite clear that the violence is meted out in an inquisitorial environment that is replete with lies and ridiculously false testimony. The
prologue pretends to tell lies, "things . . . never heard nor seen"
("cosas . . . nunca oídas ni vistas," 91/*xvii*), in the same manner that
servants are commonly known to lie to their masters: "But ask Your
Grace if it bothers him when they tell him. . . . What would he do
if it were true? And everything goes like this so. . . . It does not
bother me that those who find pleasure in it take part in it and enjoy
it." ("Mas pregunten a su merced si le pesa cuando le dicen. . . .
¿Que hiciera si fuera verdad? Y todo va desta manera que. . . . No
me pesara que hayan parte y se huelguen con ello todos los que en
ella algún gusto hallaren," 88–89/*xviii*; note the linking verb *pesar*).
Lazaro lies to the squire who, in turn, describes how he would lie to
the master he hopes to find, just like those who serve the nobility
are known to lie: "dissembling the best I knew how" ("disimulando
lo mejor que pude," 132/38); "I would know how to lie to him as well
as anybody else" ("Yo sabría mentille tan bien como otro," 151/56). In
fact, the text abounds in lies, and there is not a single *tratado* that
does not treat of deception in some form. It would come as no surprise to any Jewish or converso reader who did not already recognize
it that Lazaro's narrative is recounted, in the tradition of Odysseus
the liar, in an environment in which a monstrous Inquisition would
burn and consume those victims who are not clever enough to blind
it: "Sant Juan y ciégale" (119/25). Whether his funny story is true or
false, the consequences for Lazaro and for those Jews and conversos
to whom his finger points would be, in the perception of most Jews
and conversos, excruciatingly serious, if not deadly. In other words,

Jews and conversos, having read the text, would understand exactly what the prologue means when it says that it would be difficult for someone who really read the book to find something to laugh about: "For it might well be that someone who reads it might just find something [God only knows what!] to please him" ("Pues podría ser que alguno que las lea halle algo que le agrade," 87/xvii).

CHAPTER 6

El Abencerraje as a Converso Text

for Samuel G. Armistead

S EVERAL PRINTED versions of the story of *El Abencerraje y la hermosa Jarifa* have survived from around the middle of the sixteenth century. There is consensus among scholars that the most artistically accomplished of these versions is the one published in 1565 in an edition of the *Inventario* of Antonio de Villegas. This version, as edited by Francisco López Estrada in 1980, will be cited in this chapter. The English translation cited, by Keller, also has Villegas' text, without modern orthography, on facing pages.

The story told by Villegas is about a well-known Spanish leader named Rodrigo de Narváez who was made mayor of two frontier towns, Antequera and Alora, in reward for his valiant efforts in conquering them for the Christians when they were occupied by the Moors. One night after supper, Rodrigo selects nine of his brave knights to accompany him on a ride along the frontier to see if they will encounter the Moorish enemy. The ten riders divide themselves equally when they reach a fork in the road and agree to signal one another by horn if necessary. The group of five traveling without their leader, Rodrigo, encounters and engages a Moorish knight who unhorses three of them before another of the five, seeing that they were no match for the Moor, blows on his horn to summon help from Rodrigo and the other four knights. When Rodrigo arrives on the scene, he sees four of his five knights on the ground and the Moor about to unhorse the fifth. He challenges the Moor to fight with him

alone, assuring him that he, Rodrigo, will surrender the entire party
of ten if the Moor defeats him.

Rodrigo succeeds in conquering the Moor, but only because the
Moor is wounded and tired from the fight before Rodrigo engaged
him. Rodrigo learns from the Moor that he is called Abindarráez
(literally, the name means "son of the military governor"), a descendant of the Abencerrajes (literally, "descendants of the saddler") who,
with the exception of the father and uncle of Abindarráez, were un-
justly executed by the king of Granada for treachery. The father and
uncle of Abindarráez were spared on condition that they raise their
children outside the city of Granada.

Abindarráez also tells Rodrigo that his own misfortune was even
greater than that of his ancestors, because when Rodrigo captured
him he was on his way to meet and marry his lover, Jarifa ("noble" in
Arabic). Rodrigo immediately offers to release his captive on condition
that he return to Rodrigo's custody within three days. Abindarráez
promises to return in three days and joins Jarifa, whom he secretly
marries without her father's permission. When he tells Jarifa why he
must leave her, she insists on accompanying him.

On their way to surrender themselves to Rodrigo in Alora, Abindarráez and Jarifa meet an old man who is on his way to do business
with Rodrigo. The old man tells them one of many stories he knows
that illustrate the virtuousness of this Rodrigo de Narváez. The old
man's story about Rodrigo was meant to illustrate that he was, in the
words of the storyteller, the most honorable and virtuous knight the
storyteller had ever seen (128/71).

According to the story, Rodrigo was madly in love with a married
woman who, because of her fidelity to her husband, paid him no
mind at first, until the husband highly praised Rodrigo to his wife as
"the most valiant and virtuous knight" that he had ever seen. Then,
seeing how much even her husband valued Rodrigo's virtue, the wife
changed her mind, and she made a tryst with Rodrigo in her husband's absence and yielded to his advances. The text is deliberately
permeable; it says that "she received him sweetly and put him in
her chamber where they exchanged very sweet words" ("le recibió
dulcemente y le metió en su cámara, donde pasaron muy dulces
palabras" 130/73), which permits the reader to conclude either that
only words were exchanged or, with double entendre, that words and
carnal love were exchanged. Then, when the lady tells Rodrigo not
to flatter himself because it was not his passion but her husband's
praise that conquered her, Rodrigo takes the high road and decides,
from that day forward, to guard her husband's honor as closely as his

own. The storyteller and Abindarráez conclude that they had never seen such virtue, but Jarifa's response is more complex; it deserves, as we shall soon see, a deeper analysis than this plot summary provides.

In Alora, Rodrigo treats Abindarráez and Jarifa as noble guests rather than as prisoners. Abindarráez asks Rodrigo to request a pardon from the King of Granada for him and Jarifa for the wrong they did by marrying secretly without the permission of Jarifa's father. Rodrigo writes the king of Granada stating that he would free the couple without ransom if the king, in turn, would pardon them. The king prevails upon Jarifa's father to forgive the couple, and the father provides the couple with a gift of money for Rodrigo. Abindarráez adds horses and weapons to the money and sends them with a gracious letter as a gift to Rodrigo. Rodrigo replies as graciously in writing, accepting the horses and the arms, but returning the money. Jarifa pronounces Rodrigo invincible in arms and courtliness, and all remain friends, the story ends, for the rest of their lives.

This story about two Spaniards, a Christian and a Moor, makes no direct reference to conversos, and yet most scholars agree that it speaks for conversos indirectly. These scholars have noticed that one version of the story contains a prologue that dedicates the work to an Aragonese nobleman, Jerónimo Jiménez de Embún, whose mother and wife were conversas; scholars also surmise that two authors who include the story in their own work, Jorge de Montemayor and Antonio de Villegas, were conversos (López Estrada 1980, 49).

The prevailing theory is that these conversos were interested in the work because, at a time when religious intolerance was being enforced in Spain by the Inquisition, the story exhorts Spain to establish a peaceful *modus vivendi* for all its citizens even though they may be of different religious persuasions, as Rodrigo de Narváez and Abindarráez had done in the story. This theory is supported in the text by the fact that the story told by Abindarráez about the persecution and exile of the *abencerrajes* of Granada is very reminiscent of the persecution and exile of the Jews of Spain: "It is surely impossible," writes one distinguished critic, "not to think of other collective disasters, like the expulsion of the Jews in 1492, of which certain Spanish readers must have been reminded by the fate of the Abencerrajes" (Guillén 1971, 195–96; see also Shipley 1978).

Although there is consensus in the criticism of *Abencerraje* that the work is an artistic piece of propaganda for the converso cause, no one has suggested, as far as I know, that the work is converso in the sense that it can be interpreted in contradictory ways. In fact, there is also consensus on the interpretation of the work. Most critics would agree with Claudio Guillén, for example, that

> the perfect knight is, of course, Rodrigo de Narváez. . . . The prestige of Narváez follows him everywhere and lifts up the spirit of all those who fight with him or against him. . . . Consequently, the Moor (who to all extents and purposes behaves like a Christian dressed as a Moor) feels obliged not only to deserve Jarifa's love, but, as a true Abencerraje, to be worthy of his friendship with Narváez. Hence a series of conflicts, as well as of self-perfecting and ennobling actions: Abindarráez, more youthful and impulsive than the mature Narváez, learns to control his own wishes and to teach Jarifa, by word and example, to master her own. Thus a kind of chain reaction takes place, leading to the final competition, in the ability for self-sacrifice and knightly generosity, between the various characters in the story, including Jarifa's father and the king of Granada (who, as the introductory paragraph promised, add a few "rasguños" to the picture). But in the final analysis, none succeeds in outdoing Rodrigo de Narváez (who learned earlier, when he was a younger man, to curb his own will and conciliate loyalty with love, as the final tale of his frustrated affair with a married woman makes clear), though they have all been guided and lifted up by his example. (Guillén 1971, 213)

In other words, the prevailing interpretation of the work is monocultural: the non-Christian Moors in the work, who behave like Christians anyway, are all made to learn the virtues of the perfect Christian knight, Rodrigo de Narváez.

The text of *El Abencerraje* certainly encourages a monocultural Christian interpretation, especially since to do otherwise in an oppressive monocultural environment would be to risk the lives of those associated with the text. But the text of *El Abencerraje* also makes clear, with a pointed reference to the parable of the sower in the Christian books of Matthew, Mark, and Luke, that it is directed to a hierarchy of readers, most of whom will capture its superficial meaning and miss its essence: "So that the essence and effect of it [virtue in a damaged subject] is like the seed that falling on good soil grows and on bad soil was lost" ("Bien que la esencia y efecto de ella es como el grano que, cayendo en buena tierra, se acrescienta, y en la mala se perdió," 103/43). In this parable of the sower, the listener who hears the story and does not understand it ranks worst in the hierarchy: "Hear the parable of the sower. When any one hears the word of the kingdom and does not understand it, the evil one comes and snatches away what is sown in his heart" (Matthew 13:18, 19).

By this Christian standard, Rodrigo and his Christian soldiers are hopelessly poor listeners. When Rodrigo hears the parable of Abindarráez' kingdom, he not only does not understand it but has absolutely no curiosity about it:

> "Knight, give yourself up for conquered, if not, I must kill you."
> "You might well be able to kill me," said the Moor, "for you have me in your power, but no one will be able to conquer me except the person who once conquered me." The governor did not stop to ponder the mystery with which these words were being said, and using at that point his customary virtue, he helped him stand up.

> —Caballero, date por vencido; si no, matarte he.
> —Matarme bien podrás—dijo el moro—que en tu poder me tienes, mas no podrá vencerme sino quien una vez me venció. El alcaide no paró en el misterio con que se decían estas palabras, y usando de su acostumbrada virtud, le ayudó a levantar. (110/49)

Shortly after this scene, Abindarráez sighs and expresses his grief in his own language, which, of course, Rodrigo and his soldiers fail completely to understand: "He heaved a big, deep sigh and gabbled a few words in Arabic that no one understood" ("Él dio un grande y profundo sospiro, y habló algunas palabras en algarabía, que ninguno entendió," 111/51). By contrast, Abindarráez and the other non-Christian characters in the story have no problem understanding Rodrigo and his soldiers, and when Jarifa expresses sufficient curiosity and is told Rodrigo's story by an old man, she understands and interprets it well. This discrepancy in the powers of understanding among the major characters of the story is sufficient justification for rereading the story from a perspective other than a monocultural Christian one, especially in the light of the parable of the sower cited in the text.

Much has been made of the lack of chronological verisimilitude in the selection of the name Rodrigo de Narváez. It has been noted correctly that the historical Rodrigo de Narváez helped in the conquest of the town of Antequera in 1410 and died in 1424, but that he could not possibly be mayor of the town of Alora, which did not fall into Christian control before 1482 (López Estrada 1980, 33). The name Narváez, however, functions prominently among the leaders of Antequera and Alora, which is probably why the author of the story of El Abencerraje uses the name Narváez. It is very likely that the name Rodrigo was kept among the Narváez family in memory of the ancestor who helped conquer Antequera in 1410, which would give the author of the fiction good reason to use it. But it is clear that the name Rodrigo is meant to function in the text not as a historical signifier of any single event in Spanish history, but rather as a historical symbol of Spain. The careful reader is therefore alerted to read *Rodrigo* in the text symbolically.

Even the least historically aware among Spanish readers must have known that the name Rodrigo served as a kind of frame for all of Spanish history up until the time of the composition of *El Abencerraje*. And few Jewish and converso readers will have ignored, as they read the name Rodrigo in the text, that it was the name of the last of the Visigothic kings of Spain, Rodrigo *el último godo*. Jews and conversos in Spain were not permitted to forget that their ancestors were responsible in part for the conquest of their country by the Moors in 711. Historians like Lucas of Tuy kept reminding Spaniards that Spain was punished by God because King Witiza favored the Jews over the Christians:

> Addidit et Uuitiza iniquitatem super iniquitatem, et Iudaeos ad Hispanias euocauit, atque fractis ecclesiarum priuilegiis Iudaeis inmunitatum priuilegia dedit. Deus autem tantum facinus, tantamque malitiam abhorrens hominum ruinam et subuersionem Hispaniarum populis intulit. (And Witiza piled iniquity upon iniquity, and he called upon the Jews in Spain, and having broken the privileges of the [Christian] churches, he gave the privileges of immunity to the Jews. As a result, abhorring such an outrage and such malice among men, God brought subversion and ruin to the people of Spain" [in Menéndez Pidal 1980, 5–6; translation mine]).

In 694, eight years before Witiza became king, the Christians had accused the Spanish Jews of plotting with the Jews of North Africa to overthrow the king of Spain. As a consequence, the seventeenth Council of Toledo decreed that all Jews were to be exiled from their homes and sent as slaves to Christian masters throughout Spain (Ashtor 1973, 13–14). When the text of *El Abencerraje* reads that the *abencerrajes* and their families were exiled because "they conspired to kill the king and divide the kingdom among themselves, in order to avenge his insult" ("se conjuraron de matar al rey y dividir el reino entre sí, vengando su injuria," 114–15/53), the intelligent reader is prompted to understand a reference not simply to the *abencerrajes* of Granada or to the Jews of Spain in 1492, but also to the Jews of Spain around the time of Rodrigo, the last Gothic king of Spain.

Witiza had undone the effect of the decree of the Council of Toledo of 694, creating the reversal of the privileges to which Lucas of Tuy refers; upon Witiza's death, Rodrigo and his supporters were determined to reinstate the harsh anti-Jewish laws, which is why Jews welcomed the coming of the Moors in 711 and collaborated with the invaders, and why the Jews were blamed in the historical and folk memories of the Spanish people as traitors to the Christian causes of the country. The reconquest of Spain, therefore, was conceived not as a reconquest from the Moors alone but from the Jews as well; the embodiment of that reconquest was another Rodrigo, Rodrigo de Vivar, el Cid campeador.

Rodrigo de Vivar, as he is portrayed in the national epic poem *El Cid,* is not only the "reconqueror" of the country from the Moors but especially, as far as the text of *El Abencerraje* is concerned, a valiant Christian capable of making and keeping valiant Moorish friends, like Abengalvón. In fact, one of the principal roles of Abengalvón in the poem is to underscore the treachery of the cruel and cowardly Infantes de Carrión, who would have been understood by listeners of the poem to be more treacherous even than a Moor. Their greed would have been perceived to have equaled or surpassed that of the Jewish moneylenders, Raquel and Vidas, whom the Cid deceives— justly, no doubt, in the eyes of many Christian listeners. So that when Rodrigo de Narváez writes declining the money sent to him by Abindarráez and Jarifa's father, lest he, Rodrigo, be perceived as a "greedy merchant" ("cobdicioso mercader," 137/81), the text intends that intelligent readers remember another Rodrigo, el de Vivar, and his negotiations with the Jewish moneylenders Raquel and Vidas. When Rodrigo de Narváez concludes his letter with the words "And also, lady, I am not accustomed to robbing ladies, but to serving them and honoring them" ("Y también, señora, yo no acostumbro robar damas, sino servirlas y honrarlas," 137/83), the intelligent reader is alerted to how the Infantes de Carrión plotted to rob the daughters of the Cid of their inheritance and to dishonor rather than serve them.

Rodrigo de Narváez, therefore, was perceived by Christians in Spain as being symbolic of the completion of the reconquest for which Rodrigo el último godo had sacrificed his life, and for which the Cid, Rodrigo de Vivar, had set the stage. For this reason Rodrigo de Narváez came to be called, in Spanish legend and history, Rodrigo el Bueno, and some Spanish writers, like the author of the epic poem entitled *The Good Spaniard* (*El buen español*), compared him with Rodrigo de Vivar (López Estrada 1957, 253–56). In comparison with these other heroes named Rodrigo, the reader of *El Abencerraje* should understand the reference to patriotic deeds that are so normal in Spain that they are taken for granted: "He performed deeds worthy of perpetual memory, except that this Spain of ours holds courage to be worth so little, because it is so native to Spain and so commonplace in her, that it seems to her that however much can be done is little" ("Hizo hechos dignos de perpetua memoria, sino que esta nuestra

España tiene en tan poco el esfuerzo, por serle tan natural y ordinario, que le paresce que cuanto se puede hacer es poco," 104–05/43).

In *El Abencerraje*, Rodrigo de Narváez is so quintessentially Spanish that the emphasis in the text's description of him, "the Spanish captain" ("el capitán español," 137/81), is intended to fall more on *español* than on *capitán*. To Jewish and converso readers, of course, this also means that the deeds worthy of perpetual memory which come so naturally to Christian Spain refer also to those repeated acts aimed directly against Jews, including those committed during the time of Rodrigo el último godo, as well as those symbolized by the deception of Raquel and Vidas by Rodrigo de Vivar, even though Jews and conversos are not mentioned directly in the text of *El Abencerraje*.

Jewish and converso readers would find reference to themselves and their ancestors not simply in the story of the persecution and exile of the *abencerrajes* of Granada, but also in the opening sentence, "The story goes that in the time of Prince Ferdinand who captured Antequera" ("Dice el cuento que en el tiempo del infante don Fernando, que ganó a Antequera," 104/43). It is well known that in the year 1410, when Rodrigo de Narváez helped Fernando win Antequera, King Martin of Aragon died; the person who most strongly influenced the selection of Fernando as king was Fray Vincent Ferrer. Fray Vincent Ferrer was, in 1410, as powerful an anti-Jewish preacher as the Archdeacon Ferrant Martinez had been nineteen years before, in 1391, when Jews throughout Spain were massacred. In January 1412, Fray Vincent Ferrer's plan against the Jews took effect in Valladolid:

> Upon his advice the Jews were forced, whenever he came to a locality, to give up their homes in the central parts of the city among the Christians. The evictions were carried out with the utmost brutality. Filthy and unsanitary quarters were assigned to the Jews, and they were ruthlessly forced out of their homes even if no other dwelling places were available for them at the moment. The monk-preacher's tour gave rise to many conversions and to the dissolution of communities that had still maintained themselves or been strengthened during the previous twenty years. (Baer 1971, II, 95, 167)

In June 1412, when Fernando was elected king, Fray Vincent Ferrer was promulgating his laws against the Jews of Aragon: "The king warned the leading citizens to treat the Jews according to their rights, as special subjects of the king, and if Maestre Vincent Ferrer made special regulations concerning the Jews, the citizens must bring them before the king for ratification" (Baer 1971, II, 170–71). There can be no question that whereas for Christian readers, the time of Fernando de Antequera was a time of triumph, these same words in *El Abencerraje* for Jewish and converso readers would evoke a time of intense pain and persecution.

But, just as the name Rodrigo de Narváez in *El Abencerraje* refers to the time of Antequera as well as to a later time after Alora was captured in 1482, so too the name Fernando refers both to 1410, when Fernando I became a contender for the throne of Aragon, and to the time around 1492 when Fernando II of Aragon, now one of the Catholic kings of Castile, completed what began with Antequera, by capturing the Moors of Granada and expelling the Jews from Spain. Fernando de Antequera is firmly linked in the history of Spain and in the text of *El Abencerraje* with Fernando el Católico. For the Christian reader of *El Abencerraje*, Antequera under Fernando I is the prelude to Granada under Fernando II. To the Jewish and converso reader, however, the conversion of thousands of Jews—as many as 200,000, according to Benzion Netanyahu (1973, 242)—during the reign of Fernando I from 1412–1416 is the prelude to the expulsion in 1492 under Fernando II, the Catholic.

Two incidents in the life of Ferdinand the Catholic recall the kind of conspiracy, hastily attributed to an entire category of people, to which the text of *El Abencerraje* refers. For the first of these incidents the Jews and conversos, in general, were blamed, and for the second, the Moors, in general, were suspected. In 1485, a number of citizens of Zaragoza appealed to Ferdinand the Catholic and to the Pope against the institution of the Spanish Inquisition in Aragon. Receiving no consideration from the king or from the Pope, they decided to take matters into their own hands and conspired to kill one of the two Inquisitors of Zaragoza; the conspirators counted on support from the people of the city, where the hatred of the Inquisition was widespread. But when the Inquisitor, Pedro Arbúes de Epila, was killed as he kneeled at prayer in a cathedral, it turned out that the people of the city hated Jews and conversos more than they despised the Inquisition:

> The populace, ignorant of the extent or ultimate object of the conspiracy, were filled with vague apprehensions of an insurrection of the new Christians, who had so often been the objects of outrage; and they could only be appeased by the archbishop of Saragossa, riding through the streets, and proclaiming that no time should be lost in detecting and punishing the assassins. . . . In the course of this persecution, two hundred individuals perished at the stake, and a

still greater number in the dungeons of the Inquisition; and there was scarcely a noble family in Aragon but witnessed one or more of its members condemned to humiliating penance in the *autos da fé*. . . . Arbues received all the honors of a martyr. His ashes were interred on the spot where he had been assassinated. A superb mausoleum was erected over them, and, beneath his effigy, a bas relief was sculptured representing his tragic death, with an inscription containing a suitable denunciation of the race of Israel. (Prescott 1893, II, 22–23; see also Lea 1906, I, 249–60)

The second incident was an attack on the life of Fernando el Católico himself on 7 December 1492. Suspecting a conspiracy, the wounded Fernando prevented his courtiers from killing the attacker. Many groups were suspected, but the perception that captured the imagination of many was one that blamed the Moors and linked the event with the murder of the Inquisitor Arbues when the Jews were blamed: "The great bell of Velilla, whose miraculous tolling always announced some disaster to the monarchy, was heard to strike at the time of this assault on Ferdinand, being the fifth time since the subversion of the kingdom by the Moors. The fourth was the assassination of the inquisitor Arbues" (Prescott 1893, II, 147).

It turned out that the attacker was a lone lunatic, a sixty-year-old peasant who believed himself to be king. The king and queen, satisfied that there was no conspiracy, would have freed the madman, but the perception persisted that he was not mad and might well have been part of a conspiracy to usurp the throne, and so the mad peasant was executed with cruel vengeance. The point is not that *El Abencerraje* refers solely and directly to these two incidents—the murder of Arbues and the attack on Fernando el Católico; the point is that, by referring to well-known names that automatically bring to mind incidents in Spanish history, the text deliberately and artistically makes the reader ponder a characteristic tendency on the part of Christians in Spain to blame other Spaniards whom they perceive as ancient enemies.

Since religion was at the root of the tendency in Spain for enemies to blame each other, the text of *El Abencerraje* repeatedly makes direct reference to the differences between religions. Rodrigo de Narváez is described as someone who has done a great deal for his king as well as for his religion: "This knight, then, did so much in the service of his faith and his king that . . ." ("Hizo pues, este caballero tanto en servicio de su ley y de su rey," 105/43). Also, the king of Granada, who admires Rodrigo alone among Christians for his virtue (132, 134), orders Jarifa's father to pardon her and her husband, Abindarráez; Jarifa's father, in turn, orders her and Abindarráez to treat Rodrigo as a friend even though their religions are different: "Hold him from now on as a friend even though the religions might be different" ("Tenedle de aquí adelante por amigo, aunque las leyes sean diferentes," 135/81). For Christian readers, this might mean that the king of Granada and Jarifa's father concede in some measure the superiority of Christianity over their own religion. For Jewish readers, however, the words "even though the religions [literally, "laws"] might be different," especially when they are read in context with the time of Fernando de Antequera, recall the tradition of disputations between Christians and Jews, as, for example, the ones held in Tortosa throughout 1413 and for most of 1414, that is, at the height of Fernando's reign (Baer 1971, II, 170–243). Indeed, for Jewish readers the entire text of *El Abencerraje* can be read as a disputation between inimical religions.

The warring religions in *El Abencerraje* have not been convincingly identified, in my opinion, especially since most critics agree that the Moors in the work behave more like Christians than like followers of Islam. The religious enemies in *El Abencerraje* are not represented by the Christian Rodrigo de Narváez on the one hand and the Moslem Abindarráez on the other. Rather, Rodrigo de Narváez and Abindarráez represent more and less virtuous followers of Neoplatonism, Christian and Islamic, and intelligent readers are left to surmise that the other religion, or "ley," is Judaism. In other words, *El Abencerraje* is written squarely in the courtly love tradition of two other texts which I have identified in my 1986 book as converso: *Cárcel de Amor* and *Celestina*. It is believed that the author of *Celestina* owned a copy of *Cárcel de Amor,* as passages in both texts seem to confirm; and López Estrada (1965, 267) has shown that a section of one of the versions of *El Abencerraje* is patterned closely after a section of *Cárcel de Amor.*

It would have taken few contemporary Jewish and converso readers by surprise that Abindarráez is portrayed as a Moorish version of the heros of *Cárcel de Amor* (Leriano), and *Celestina* (Calisto). Jarifa's role, however, is significantly different from that of the heroines, Laureola and Melibea, in *Cárcel de Amor* and *Celestina*. Laureola is the goddess-like woman for whom Leriano pines and dies after tearing up her letters, placing the pieces in a glass of water, and drinking them. Melibea is the woman Calisto calls his God. In both *Cárcel de*

Amor and *Celestina,* the Jewish reader is supposed to deduce that
Christianity is an idolatrous religion, and that, therefore, Judaism is
superior (see Nepaulsingh 1986, 174–200). Although she too is a kind
of goddess, as we shall see, Jarifa's role in *El Abencerraje* is mainly
to determine which of the two courtly lovers, the Christian Rodrigo
or the Moslem Abindarráez, is the more virtuous Neoplatonist. Once
the more virtuous of the two is determined, the Jewish and converso
reader has little difficulty deciding how the higher of the two forms
of Neoplatonism compares with Judaism.

The attentive reader is alerted to the text's status as a debate
between three discordant religions not simply by the reference to
different religions, but especially by Abindarráez' statement that Jarifa seemed to him "more beautiful than Venus when she went out to
the contest for the apple" ("Parescióme en aquel punto más hermosa
que Venus cuando salió al juicio de la manzana," 118/59). In *La Diana,*
by the way, there is a similar reference to the judgment of Paris
(another reason overlooked by scholars for the insertion of the *Abencerraje* into *La Diana,* and for the artistic compatibility of the two
texts); *La Diana,* too, is about a debate between the three religions,
as we shall see in the next chapter.

The twentieth-century reader might be struck by the persistence
of these debates between Judaism, Christianity, and Islam, especially
since they are almost as old as Christianity and Islam themselves, and
since they keep repeating the same arguments and counterarguments
without apparent hope of resolution; the history of these debates
has been sensitively documented by the noted Christian religious
historian Jaroslav Pelikan. At all periods there have been those who
held the debates to be futile. There were even Jews who firmly believed that the massacre of 1391 and the edict of expulsion were
punishments from God because Spanish Jews insisted on debating
points of religion with the Christians, contrary to Jewish law. An
Italian Jew living around 1492 wrote:

> I heard that the bitter persecutions of 1391 in Catalonia were caused
> by the desire of the Jews to have disputations with the Christians.
> Finally, when the latter found themselves vanquished, they arose and
> killed them. Many, almost all, were then baptized, and gave up their
> faith. From this persecution resulted that of 1492, when the Spanish
> king exiled nearly six hundred thousand persons. Many of them died
> on the way, and in the vessels, but more were baptized. The afore-
> mentioned king saw that the Jews of his country taught the Marranos
> the Torah, and he thought: Once I expel the Jews, all the Marranos
> in my kingdom—and the country is full of them—will become real
> Christians. And so it was. All this happened to them because they

did not observe the covenant of our forefathers, and the teachings of the sages, who advised against disputations on questions of faith. (Marx, 81)

The quotation is interesting, even if it contains inaccuracies, because it shows how deeply the events of 1391 and 1492 remained indelibly impressed upon the mind of Jews, even outside the borders of the Spanish peninsula.

Perhaps there were those who believed that debates would lead to peaceful coexistence. Others would have known that the debates, in which Jews were often "commanded to participate," were a trap; Pelikan's summary for an earlier period fits fifteenth-century Spain as well:

> Behind the treatises, at least in many cases, were actual disputations between Christian theologians and Jewish rabbis, disputations in which the Jews were commanded to participate. There seems to have been an effort to establish rules of procedure for such debates, as in the admonition that neither party should ridicule or blaspheme the faith of the other or tread upon consciences or conceal the truth. Although fairness may have made such rules necessary, the purpose of the encounter was undeniable: to convert the Jews to Christianity. When a Jew suggested that there should be a mutual recognition of one another's faith, with no attempt to proselytize, his Christian opponent rejected the suggestion, arguing that it was to the Jew's benefit to surrender his vain and empty creed in favor of Christian belief. (Pelikan 1974, 202)

In fifteenth-century Spain, too, as in the time Pelikan describes in the above passage, Jews were baited into debates. But once the edict of expulsion made debates irrelevant in 1492, it is natural to expect that some members of the oppressed culture would seek to express their resistance in documents like converso texts that attempt to assert, with artistically coded subtlety, the superiority of their religion.

The *Abencerraje* has been analyzed often enough for its Neoplatonic content, so I will not repeat that analysis here, except to make a minor but important adjustment to the understanding of the key first paragraph to the work. The prevailing interpretation of that first paragraph is represented in the long quotation from Guillén above. According to that interpretation, the work is a live portrait of virtue ("un vivo retrato de virtud," 103) in which Rodrigo, the Christian, is a perfect knight who teaches lessons in virtue to the other characters, especially to Abindarráez and to Jarifa. This is a valid reading of the text from a Christian perspective. From a proper Neoplatonic perspective, however, the word *retrato* means "portrait" only insofar as a portrait, even a live portrait, is a mere reflection, a lower image of ideal virtue. The Neoplatonic concept of the "universe as a graduated hierarchy of images" (Pelikan, 120) had infiltrated Judaism, Christianity, and Islam. It is reflected, for example, in a passage from Saint Paul's second letter to the Corinthians that distinguishes between Jewish and Christian ways of interpreting: "But we all [i.e., Christians], with open face beholding as in a glass the glory of the Lord, are changed into the same image from glory to glory even as by the spirit of the Lord" (2 Cor. 3:18).

Passages with similar hierarchical arrangements of images between ideal and real poles can be found in the *Dialogues of Love* by the Jewish Neoplatonist, Leon Hebreo, as well as in the texts of many Islamic Neoplatonists like al-Farabi and Ibn Sina. This means that the first paragraph of *Abencerraje* also says that Rodrigo is not a perfect knight but a mere reflection of perfect Christian virtue; he is, in other words, like all the other characters in the work, a damaged subject ("dañado subjecto," 103) in which the perfect gem of virtue is set. For a Neoplatonic interpretation of the work as a whole, this also means that, contrary to current valid but incomplete interpretations, Rodrigo does not teach any of the other characters anything at all. In fact, Rodrigo is inferior to Abindarráez and to Jarifa when the work is read from the perspective of Jarifa, the noble judge.

The judgment concerning Rodrigo that is normally cited to prove his superiority is in Jarifa's comment, "Whoever thinks of conquering Rodrigo de Narváez in arms and courtesy thinks wrong" ("Quien pensare vencer a Rodrigo de Narváez de armas y cortesía pensará mal," 137/83). Critics have failed to see that although Jarifa praises Rodrigo for his skill at fighting and at courteous diplomacy ("armas y cortesía"), she deliberately omits the trait for which Rodrigo is best known: virtue. In fact, Jarifa had already judged Rodrigo for his alleged virtue and found him wanting.

After Jarifa had listened to the old man's story about Rodrigo, and after Abindarráez and the old man had concluded from the story that Rodrigo was the most virtuous knight they had ever seen (128/71), Jarifa's contrary judgment is sarcastic and devastating:

> She replied, "My God, sir, I would never wish a lover with that kind of virtue, but he must have been in love only a little bit, because he fell out of it so quickly, and the husband's honor could do more with him than the woman's beauty." And she said other very witty words about this.

Ella respondió:—Por Dios, señor, yo no quisiera servidor tan virtu-
oso, mas él debía estar poco enamorado, pues tan presto salió afuera
y pudo más con él la honra del marido que la hermosura de la mujer.
Y sobre esto dijo otras muy graciosas palabras. (131/73)

Again the text is deliberately and artistically permeable, like a
filigree. Jarifa's words might be taken to mean, to her discredit, from
a perspective other than Neoplatonic, be it Christian, Jewish, or Islamic, that she would have preferred her lover to have pursued his
illicit physical passion. But from a Neoplatonic perspective, the person discredited is Rodrigo, whose love is based on physical passion
(and so is quickly spent) rather than on the Neoplatonic reflection of
ideal beauty. By contrast, the love of Abindarráez for Jarifa is based
on the Neoplatonic contemplation of the reflection of pure beauty,
and is not consummated until after a solemn though secret marriage
ceremony. Abindarráez repeats that he was "conquered by [Jarifa's]
beauty" ("vencido de su hermosura," 116/55), that he feels obligated
only to her beauty ("a mí sola vuestra hermosura me obliga," 117/57),
and he wonders if when he is removed from the reflection of her
beauty she will remember him ("Apartándose vuestra hermosura de
mí, ¿ternéis alguna vez memoria deste vuestro captivo?" 119/61). Perhaps the most important aspect of Neoplatonic love is beauty. Neoplatonists argued that the difference between true love and false is that
false love disappears with carnal consummation or with absence,
whereas the beauty of the beloved captures a true lover forever and
leads through contemplation first to the reflection then to the real
love of God.

The text leaves little doubt that Jarifa judges Abindarráez superior
in virtuous love to Rodrigo: her words in judgment of Rodrigo are
patterned after and meant to supersede Rodrigo's judgment of Abindarráez. After listening to Abindarráez' story, Rodrigo had said, "Abindarráez, I want you to see that my virtue can do more than your
ruinous fortune" ("Abindarráez, quiero que veas que puede más mi
virtud que tu ruin fortuna," 122/63); mimicking his words victoriously
and rejecting his type of virtue, Jarifa said of Rodrigo, "The husband's
honor could do more with him than the woman's beauty" (73). The
same verb of measurement ("poder [hacer] más," to be able [to do]
more) is used in both judgments and, by Neoplatonic standards, Rodrigo fails because he values honor above beauty, whereas Abindarráez feels obligated only to the beauty of Jarifa.

Although the text of the *Abencerraje* intends to make clear with
Jarifa's witty words that Islam, as represented by a Neoplatonic Moorish knight, is superior to Christianity, as represented by a perfect

Spanish courtly lover, it also attempts to make clear to the Jewish and converso reader that Christianity and Islam are alike, and that both are inferior to Judaism. Whether or not Rodrigo consummated his passion for the once faithful wife with words or with carnal love, he is, in either event, guilty of breaking the commandment not to covet one's neighbor's wife; he is, in Orthodox eyes, an adulterer. Both Rodrigo and Abindarráez break another key commandment. For Abindarráez, Jarifa becomes not merely a reflection of true beauty, but an icon he wears either on the sleeve of his burnoose or tattooed on his right arm itself. The text is, once again, artistically permeable: "He carried his right arm [stretched straight] behind [his back] and on it was wrought a beautiful lady" ("Traía el brazo derecho rezagado y labrada en él una hermosa dama," 107/47). It is on this same right arm that Rodrigo inflicts the decisive wound that conquers Abindarráez (110/49).

Scholars have noted the symbolism of making Abindarráez vulnerable where he wears Jarifa, but the symbolism has not been well explained. There can be no escaping the religious symbolism of the skirmish: when one Christian attacks Abindarráez, the Moor wins easily, the text says, because "the Moor knew more about that art" ("el moro sabía más de aquel menester," 109/47); that is to say, especially from a Jewish point of view, Moors know more about one God than Christians do. When three of the remaining four Christians attack the single Moor in vain, the text emphasizes the words *Christians* and *Moor:* "So that now against the Moor there were three Christians, each of whom was sufficient [to fight] ten Moors, and all together they were no match for this one [Moor] alone" ("de manera que ya contra el moro eran tres cristianos, que cada uno bastaba para diez moros, y todos juntos no podían con este solo," 109/47). From a Jewish perspective, this passage says that the Christians' vulnerability is the concept of the Trinity.

But then, why does the Christian win? It is not sufficient an explanation, in terms of religious symbolism, that Rodrigo fights a weakened Abindarráez and wins. Although he wins the physical battle, the text implies that Rodrigo loses the spiritual battle: Abindarráez's physical wounds are so insignificant that when he has his mainly spiritual encounter with Jarifa, neither of them pays attention to the wounds. In fact, it is not until days after that Rodrigo is made to ask, in Jarifa's presence, about the wounds he had inflicted on Abindarráez, and Abindarráez confirms that the physical wounds are nothing when compared to the spiritual wounds he escaped from Jarifa: "Lady, someone who has escaped yours will hold other wounds to be slight;

the truth is that from the skirmishes the other night I came away with two small wounds, and the journey and not having taken care of myself will probably have done me some harm" ("Señora, quien escapó de las vuestras, en poco terná otras; verdad es que de las escaramuzas de la otra noche saqué dos pequeñas heridas, y el camino y no haberme curado me habrán hecho algún daño," 132/75). In other words, Rodrigo's physical Christian prowess, when pitted against Abindarráez' spiritual defenses, amounts to little. Rodrigo's own surgeon is made to confirm that the wounds on Islam amount to nothing: "que no era nada" (132).

What, then, is the coded meaning of Rodrigo's Christian victory over Abindarráez' right Islamic arm? To understand the religious code in this part of the *Abencerraje*, one must take recourse to the clichés of the medieval debates among Christianity, Islam, and Judaism. In those debates, one of Islam's most vulnerable points was ignorance of the Virgin Mary.

> The extent of Mohammed's ignorance on the subject of the Virgin Mary could be gauged also from his mistaken supposition that the Christian Trinity consisted of Father, Mother, and Son. Further evidence came from the Koran's identification of Mary, the mother of Christ, with Miriam, the sister of Moses—a confusion on which Christian critics frequently commented. (Pelikan, 241)

Insofar as they are treated as goddesses by their lovers, Abindarráez, Leriano, and Calisto, and insofar as the women are placed in gardens reminiscent of the depiction of the Virgin Mary as a "garden enclosed," there can be little doubt that Jarifa, Laureola in *Cárcel de Amor*, and Melibea in *Celestina*, are meant to be types for the Virgin Mary. Abindarráez calls Jarifa a "beautiful goddess" ("hermosa diosa," 56/57). When Abindarráez is wounded on his right arm where he wears Jarifa as his goddess, the meaning of the religious code is that Christianity has wounded Islam at one of its most vulnerable points, that is, ignorance of the Virgin Mary. From a Jewish point of view, however, Christianity's victory over Islam on the question of the Virgin Mary is irrelevant because it proves that both Christianity and Islam are idolatrous religions.

Another cliché in the debates among the three religions was that Islam venerated Mary to a greater extent than did Christianity:

> The fact remains that "there is nothing else in all the Koran to parallel the warmth with which Christ and his mother are spoken of. Christ is represented as a unique being, but his mother's personality appears

more vividly. The Koran inspires a devotion to Mary of which Muslims might have made more" [in their debates]. When Christians, in response to Islam, emphasized the role of the Virgin in Old Testament prophecy, they were, at least in part, attaching their Mariology to that of the Koran. They [the Christians] had to admit that "in the entire Koran there do not occur any praises of Mohammed or of his mother Aminah, such as are found about Jesus and Mary." (Pelikan, 241)

When the text of the *Abencerraje* makes Abindarráez' icon of Jarifa stand out so conspicuously, it means to refer to the tradition represented in the medieval religious debates that showed Islam as more devoted to Mary than Christianity was. From an Orthodox Jewish point of view, of course, this means that Islam is more idolatrous than Christianity, according to the text of *Abencerraje*, because the medieval Jewish reader knew that, in these debates, Jews accused the other religions of idolatry so often that iconoclasm became almost coterminous with Judaism:

The iconoclastic controversy was an especially appropriate context for the use of such epithets as "Judaizer." Not only was the campaign against icons attributed to Jewish instigation, but the Christian worship of the icons was evidently one of the subjects to which the Jewish interlocutors in the Jewish-Christian dialogues recurred most often. To the orthodox [Christians], therefore, an iconoclast was simply "one with a Jewish mind." (Pelikan, 201)

From the perspective of the Jewish and converso reader, therefore, Abindarráez, with his idol so prominent and vulnerable on his arm, is guilty of idol worship. But the text of the *Abencerraje* is also insistent on linking Islamic idolatry with that of Christianity; Rodrigo is made to declare, in his final letter to Jarifa, as a final coded condemnation of himself, his intent to build a statue as a monument to himself and his descendants:

Beautiful Jarifa: Abindarráez has not been willing to let me enjoy the real triumph of his imprisonment, which consists of forgiving and doing good; and since in this country never has there been afforded me an undertaking so noble and so magnanimous and so worthy of a Spanish captain, I should like to enjoy it all and make of it a statue for my posterity and descendants.

Hermosa Jarifa: No ha querido Abindarráez dejarme gozar del veradero triumpho de su prisión, que consiste en perdonar y hacer bien; y como a mí en esta tierra nunca se me ofresció empresa tan generosa ni tan digna de capitán español, quisiera gozarla toda y labrar de ella una estatua para mi posteridad y descendencia. (137/81)

Jewish and converso readers are left with the inevitable conclusion, according to the laws of their religion and the text of the *Abencerraje*, that both Islam and Christianity are idolatrous religions and that, therefore, Judaism is superior to the other two religions of Spain.

Many of the passages that are key to deciphering the coded text of the *Abencerraje* are found only in the version included in Antonio de Villegas's *Inventory,* and not, for example, in the version inserted into *La Diana*. Critics have normally assumed, therefore, that these additions were made by Villegas and were not known to Montemayor; this is one possibility, but not the only one. It is also possible, for example, that Montemayor knew a version with these passages but edited them out of *La Diana,* perhaps because they exposed too much of the code, or perhaps for some other reason. In any event, the absence of these passages in some versions does not affect the claims made in this chapter, except to prove that there were Jewish and converso readers who interpreted the *Abencerraje* in favor of Judaism, the way the witty text of Antonio de Villegas permits.

CHAPTER 7

The Seven Books of *La Diana*

for Harriet Goldberg

Toward the end of the 1550s, there appeared in Spain a little book of complicated love stories entitled *Los siete libros de la Diana* (*The Seven Books of Diana*). Today the book reads like a script that would promptly be purchased and adapted for a television soap-opera audience. As a twentieth-century soap opera, it would probably be as successful as it was throughout Europe from the middle of the sixteenth century to the end of the seventeenth.

Between 1559 and 1699, there were twenty editions of *La Diana* in Spain. More significantly, fifty-two editions and translations (twenty Spanish editions plus thirty-two translations) were published outside of Spain, in Italy, Holland, Portugal, Switzerland, France, Germany, and England (López Estrada 1962, *lxxxvii–ciii*).

Some of this interest in *La Diana* abroad was due, no doubt, to its popular appeal and, as well, to an overriding interest at that time, throughout the Western World, in all things Spanish. Because of its encounter with a world unknown to Europe, Spain was at the center of European attention after 1492. But clearly, another deciding factor in the production of so many editions and translations of *La Diana* and books like it outside of Spain must have been the demand created by communities of Spaniards of Jewish descent forced to leave Spain after the riots of 1391 and again after the edict of expulsion in 1492. Spanish expatriates would naturally be interested in reading love stories written in Spanish; it would also be natural for most Spanish expatriates of Jewish descent and their relatives to show special inter-

103

est in reading texts that addressed the experience of Jews and conversos in Spain.

It is normal to assume that Jews and conversos in and out of Spain would derive a great deal of satisfaction from reading a text that was written in such a cleverly coded way as to elude the Spanish Inquisition while at the same time remaining patent to Jewish and converso readers. And, in fact, *La Diana* has succeeded not simply in providing satisfaction to those sixteenth- and seventeenth-century readers who were most capable of decoding it, but it has also succeeded in baffling literary experts for over four hundred years.

Most critics agree that the work is a literary masterpiece, and they have attributed its popularity to the fact that it treats of love in an ideal pastoral setting, tells true stories about contemporary courtiers, has philosophic passages about Neoplatonic humanism, has references to Greek and Roman mythology, and carries a profoundly adaptable Christian message. While all these interpretations are acceptable to most critics, there is also widespread agreement that they do not explain *La Diana* satisfactorily and that the work remains essentially enigmatic.

Critics have accepted that the author of *La Diana* might have been of Jewish descent, but they have remained divided about whether or not he was a sincere or forced convert to Christianity. I know of no acceptable way of proving an author's sincerity in religious matters, especially in times of religious persecution. Rather than attempt to establish the author's religiosity, I prefer to persuade readers that *La Diana* is a converso text; although it was written to be appreciated by Christian readers, the text also contains codes that would have been understood by many Jewish and converso readers.

Indeed, for over four hundred years, it has been easy for scholars, even those who suspected that the author was of Jewish descent, to miss most of the carefully coded Jewish and converso clues that are, of vital necessity, not on the surface of the plot, but hidden subtly among the details. Scholars working from a Christian perspective have been able to point out that although the Christian God is not mentioned unambiguously in the text, the book was easily interpreted as a profoundly Christian work; in fact, Christian sequels, like the *Clara Diana a lo divino* by Father Bartolomé Ponce, were written in imitation of it. A nonpagan God is mentioned rarely in *La Diana*. The reference occurs twice at least with the qualifier *solo*, meaning "alone" or "only," but giving the impression also that the writer would have preferrred to write "*un* solo Dios," meaning "*one* God alone": "por solo el amor de Dios" ("for the love of God alone," or "only for the love of God," 197), and "está en manos de solo Dios" ("it is in the hands of only God," or "it is in the hands of God alone," 223). The insertion of *solo* in a text like *La Diana* makes it doubtful whether the Christian or the Jewish God is being invoked.

Scholars working from a humanist perspective have been able to point to the Neoplatonic underpinnings and to the frequent use of Greek and Roman mythology in the work. Likewise, scholars working from the commonsense perspective of realism have found it easy to remind readers of the author's claim that the stories were disguised but true, and that the work was understood as a *roman à clef*. While all of these scholarly claims have merit, it is also undeniable, as I hope to show after the plot summary, that from the perspective of a Jewish or converso reader, the work was written in defiance of its inquisitorial environment.

I choose to retell the plot in summary, book by book, even at the risk of infuriating the few scholars who work with *La Diana* constantly, so that the reader who knows little or nothing about the work would appreciate how unlikely it seems, on the surface, that such a story would have anything at all to do with Jews and conversos and the Inquisition in Spain. Before the beginning of Book 1, a narrator summarizes the book's principal argument in one short paragraph. There lived on the banks of the river Ezla, in the Spanish province of León, a beautiful shepherdess named Diana who returned the love shown to her by the shepherd Sireno and rejected the love professed to her by the shepherd Sylvano, whom she hated. Sireno was forced to leave the kingdom for reasons beyond his control, and while he was away, Diana, saddened by his absence, agreed to marry Delio. Sireno, returning after one year's absence and yearning to see his beloved Diana, learns before he meets her that she is married. The paragraph ends by announcing the beginning of Book 1 and by alerting the reader that the other books contain "many diverse stories, of events that have really happened, although they go disguised under names and pastoral style" ("muy diversas hystorias, de casos que verdaderamente an sucedido, aunque van disfraçados debaxo de nombres y estilo pastoril," 7/50).

In Book 1, the shepherd Sireno, speaking to himself as he reaches the spot on the riverbank where he first saw Diana, remembers aloud how Diana used to swear to him that nothing in the world, not even the will of her parents, could make her forget him. Sireno takes out a lock of Diana's hair that he carries in his bosom and he sings a lament to it; he finds a letter that she had written him, and the narrator shares its contents with the reader. As Sireno comments on the letter, his rival for Diana's love, the shepherd Sylvano, appears, and both shepherds analyze their experience with Diana in prose and song. Sireno and Sylvano are soon joined by the shepherdess Selvagia, who knows their story. Selvagia speaks so authoritatively about love that Sireno asks her to tell her own story, which occupies most of Book 1.

Selvagia's soap opera story is complicated to the point of absurdity: Selvagia fell in love with Ismenia, a woman who lied to her saying that she was a man. Ismenia and Alanio were lovers and look-alike cousins; they planned to deceive Selvagia by letting Alanio, instead of Ismenia, meet with Selvagia. But the deception backfires on Ismenia when Alanio falls in love with Selvagia. To regain Alanio's love, Ismenia feigns love for Montano; it works, and the four lovers become locked in an interminable chase of unrequited love for one another when Montano, disregarding Ismenia's attentions, falls in love with Selvagia. Alanio kept chasing Ismenia who kept chasing Montano who kept chasing Selvagia who kept chasing Alanio. Alanio summarized the crazy situation in a song whose refrain went "Crazy love, oh, crazy love! / I for you and you for someone else" ("Amor loco, ¡ay, amor loco! / Yo por vos y vos por otro," 57/79). This interminable chase was ended when Selvagia's father removed her from her village and took her to live with his sister near Sireno and Sylvano. While there, Selvagia learns that Montano married Ismenia and Alanio married Ismenia's sister, Sylvia. At the end of Book 1, the three shepherds (Sireno, Sylvano, and Selvagia), having now shared their stories, agree to meet on the same spot the following day.

Just as the bulk of Book 1 is concerned mainly with a new character, Selvagia, and her story added to that of the main characters, so also Book 2 adds the story of a new character, Felismena, to the stories of Sireno, Sylvano, and Selvagia. When Sireno, Sylvano, and Selvagia meet the next day, as agreed, they overhear three nymphs of the goddess Diana singing the story of Sireno and Diana. Suddenly, three horrible, ugly wild men appear out of the woods and tie up the three nymphs, intending to rape them. Sireno, Sylvano, and Selvagia attack the wild men with stones and slingshots, but the shepherds are not able to overcome the wild men until Felismena, a big, strong, and beautiful shepherdess in male disguise, appears and kills all three wild men with her bow and arrows. The nymphs ask Sireno, Sylvano, and Selvagia to go to the village for food, and while they are gone, they ask Felismena to tell them her story. This takes up the greater part of Book 2.

When Felismena was still in her mother's womb, her parents had an argument about the legend of the Judgment of Paris. Felismena's mother, Delia, sided with Minerva, and her father, Andronio, with Venus. That night, the two goddesses appeared to Delia in her dreams, Venus to rebuke her, and Minerva to reward her with the news that she would bear twins, a son and daughter, both of whom would be more skillful at arms than anyone before them. Delia died in childbirth, and a few days after, Andronio died of grief. The twins were raised in a monastery where their aunt was the abbess. At the age of twelve, Felismena's brother was sent to the Portuguese court and Felismena was sent to live with one of her grandmothers.

When she was seventeen, Felismena was seen in her grandmother's garden by a high-ranking young nobleman, Don Felix, who wooed and finally won her love. When Don Felix's father learned of the love affair, he sent his son to the faraway court of a princess. Rather than suffer eternally in her lover's absence, Felismena disguised herself as a man and went in search of Don Felix. Before she found him, Felismena learned from his servant that Don Felix was madly in love with a lady of the court, Celia. Felismena joined Don Felix's household as a male servant, and in that capacity, unrecognized by Don Felix, she was asked by him to take love letters to Celia. Celia fell in love with Felismena, thinking she was a man. When Felismena failed to return Celia's love, Celia threatened to take her own life and did, in fact, die. When Don Felix heard of Celia's death, he disappeared, telling nobody of his whereabouts. Felismena disguised herself as an armed male shepherd and wandered the country in search of Don Felix; she had been doing this for two years when she saved the nymphs of Diana as well as Sireno, Sylvano, and Selvagia from the three horrible wild men.

When Felismena finished telling her story, Sireno, Sylvano, and Selvagia, singing laments of unrequited love, returned from their trip to the village for food. After dinner, one of the nymphs, Polydora, invited the entire company of unrequited lovers to go with her to the temple of the goddess Diana, at the palace of the wise Felicia, who possessed a cure for their amatory disease. At the end of Book 2, the three nymphs of Diana began to lead the other four characters toward the palace of Felicia.

At the beginning of Book 3, the pilgrims stop to spend the night at a shepherd's hut on an islet in a stream. Here they meet the beautiful Belisa, whose story takes up most of this book. Belisa was born in a village not far from where the pilgrims met her. There the widower Arsenio fell in love with her and asked his son, Arsileo, a student and poet, to compose and take poetic love letters to her.

Belisa fell in love with the son. One night when Belisa and Arsileo were together, he up a tree in her father's garden under her window, and she in her room at the window, Arsileo's father came by to woo Belisa, and, seeing her talking to a man in the dark, in a fit of jealousy he returned home for his bow and sent an arrow through the heart of the man, not knowing it was his son, Arsileo. When he found out that he had killed his son, Arsenio thrust his sword through his own heart. Belisa fled from her parents' home immediately; she had spent six months in grief and seclusion without seeing anyone when the pilgrims came upon her. At the end of Book 3, Dorida, one of the nymphs of Diana, persuaded Belisa to join the other unfortunate lovers in their pilgrimage for a cure at the temple of Diana.

With Book 4 begins the remedy for the maladies of love described in the first three books. On their way to Felicia's palace and its temple of Diana, the shepherds and shepherdesses tell their stories to Belisa. At the palace, the company is greeted by Felicia who thanks those who had helped rescue the nymphs of Diana and assures them that their ills will be remedied. Felicia directs that the nymphs dress Felismena in the garb of a courtly lady, and all express wonder at Felismena's beauty.

Felicia instructs the nymphs to give the company a tour of the temple of Diana where they see carved lessons from the history of Greece and Rome and Spain. Then the company meets the legendary Orpheus, who sings them a long epic song praising many chaste and virtuous women of Spain and Portugal. Afterward the company divides itself, in a pleasant meadow, into groups of two or three to discuss philosophical questions of love in such a way that all could hear each other without having to interrupt the conversation of another group. Sireno asks why, if it is supposed to stem from reason, love is the most ungovernable passion in the world; Felicia gives him a long reply that, like most of this section of *La Diana*, is a paraphrase of *The Dialogues of Love*, a book by Leon Hebreo (referred to in chapter 6) published in Italian in 1535. Sylvano exchanges ideas with the nymph Polydora about why lovers persist in a love that is so cruel to them; Selvagia and Belisa receive replies from the nymph Cinthia and from Felicia to their question about how absence can make people forget love. In many versions of *La Diana* published after 1561, at the end of Book 4 the entire story of *El Abencerraje y la hermosa Jarifa* is included as a tale told by Felismena at Felicia's request.

In Book 5, the remedy for unrequited love is administered by Felicia in the form of a potion that induces a deep sleep that erases the memory of love, and a book that when touched, has the power to rouse the sleeper. When Sireno is awakened from his curative nap, he no longer loves Diana. When Sylvano and Selvagia are awakened, they find out that they love each other more deeply than they had loved, respectively, Diana and Alanio. Felicia explains to Felismena and Belisa that she will not give them the potion because greater happiness is soon to befall them. She tells Felismena to leave the palace in the same armed disguise in which she went there, but this time as a shepherdess, not as a shepherd. Soon Felismena meets Arsileo, Belisa's lover who was supposed to have been killed by his father. Arsileo explains to Felismena that a necromancer who was in love with Belisa had staged an illusion that made it appear that Arsenio had killed his son. After Belisa left, Arsenio retired to a life free of worldly cares, and his son Arsileo went looking for Belisa, remaining always faithful to her. Felismena gives Arsileo directions to Felicia's palace, where he is reunited with Belisa. Sireno, Sylvano, and Selvagia meet Diana, who makes her first appearance in person in the work. Diana learns that Sireno and Sylvano are free from loving her.

In Book 6, Felismena settles a love dispute between Amarílida, the shepherdess in whose hut Arsileo was staying, and Filemón, a shepherd who is deeply in love with Amarílida, but is needlessly jealous of her relationship with Arsileo. At the end of Book 6, Sireno, Sylvano, and Selvagia meet Diana again, and it is confirmed beyond reasonable doubt that Diana has no hold on her former suitors.

In Book 7, Felismena leaves Amarílida and Filemón in Spain. She travels to the outskirts of a very beautiful city in Portugal where she meets two shepherdesses and a shepherd: Armia, Duarda, and Danteo. Armia tries to convince Duarda that she ought to return Danteo's love even though Danteo, now widowed, has acceded to his father's request that he marry someone else. As Felismena is about to intervene in the dispute between Duarda and Danteo, just as she had intervened successfully between Amarílida and Filemón, they hear the sound of fighting nearby. When they arrive at the scene of combat, they see a single knight fighting against three others. The lone knight fights bravely and had killed one of the three combatants, but the other two would certainly have killed him if Felismena had not intervened to kill one of them. The knight would have finished off the third without help, but Felismena again saved him the trouble by sending one of her arrows through the heart of the third assailant.

When the lone knight lifts his visor to thank her, Felismena recognizes her lover, Don Felix. When Don Felix realizes who has saved his life, he falls unconscious at Felismena's feet. Felismena despairs that Don Felix is dead, when the nymph Dorida appears with a cup of gold and another of silver. Dorida pours water from the silver cup over Don Felix's face, and he revives and drinks the water from the gold cup. He is thus healed instantly from the wounds of battle inflicted on him by the three attackers, and also from the wounds of love inflicted on him by Celia. Don Felix apologizes to Felismena, and she accepts his apology. The nymph Dorida invites Don Felix and Felismena to return to the temple of Diana, where the wise Felicia is awaiting them. On their way, Felismena tells Don Felix all the stories in the book. At the temple of Diana, the three reunited couples are married in Sireno's presence: Sylvano to Selvagia, Belisa to Arsileo, and Felismena to Felix. The work ends with a promise from the author to tell the rest of the stories about Sireno, Danteo, and Duarda in a sequel that, as far as we know, he never wrote.

After reading *La Diana*, the careful reader is alerted to the fact that, in its very title, the book plays with contrary meanings. The "Diana" in the title refers to two characters in the work: a shepherdess by that name who is one of the central characters in the story, also to the Roman goddess of the hunt and of chastity. The shepherdess Diana is the opposite of the goddess Diana because she accedes to her father's wish that she marry someone she does not love, whereas the goddess Diana, according to Roman mythology, obtained permission from her father never to marry.

The shepherdess and the goddess represent another contrast: the shepherdess Diana's faithlessness concerns three men, Sireno, Sylvano, and Delio, while the goddess Diana and her helpers set lovers on the path to faithfulness to one love. The title's reference to Diana thus underscores the main theme of the book from a Jewish perspective: *aliyah*, the holy pilgrimage to the one and only true love in the temple of Jerusalem, for which the temple of Diana described at the very center of the book is a secret code. The shepherdess Diana is prohibited entry into the temple of Diana because she is not chaste; that is, she did not remain faithful to her first love. As the portal to Felicia's palace explains, only "if he has not lost his first faith, / and he has kept that first love / can he enter the temple of Diana." The original text makes the equivalence between faith (*fe*) and love (*amor*) unmistakably clear: "Y si la fe primera no a perdido / y aquel primer amor a conservado / entrar puede en el templo de Diana" (165/146). For Jewish and converso readers, this means that *Los siete libros de la Diana* is first and foremost about the struggle to remain chaste, that is, faithful to their first faith. From the perspective of a Jewish or converso reader, all the classical mythology, the realistic courtly trappings, and the symbolic Christian philosophical humanism prevalent in the work (and amply described in academic criticism) are a disguise to deceive the Inquisition.

The "seven books" referred to in the title are what we would call today chapters. The fact that they are called books reminds us that *La Diana* is an important forerunner of the modern novel. Some Jewish and converso readers would also have noticed that Felicia awakens the sick lovers from their curative sleep by touching them with a book, and they would have interpreted this book as the "seven books" in the title. For these readers, this powerful book, which is also seven books, that cures all the world's ills would be the seven books of the Talmud/Torah, the Five Books of Moses and the Mishnah and Gemara. Although many rabbis forbade it, the practice was widespread, even among some rabbis, to touch a sick person with the Torah in order to affect a cure, especially if the disease was deemed a disease of the soul:

> When an infant was ill and could not sleep, or a woman was convulsed in labor pains, the Scroll was brought in and laid upon the sufferer to alleviate the pain. Of course, the religionists clamored against such impiety; some were willing to permit such practices only in case a life was in danger; others permitted the Scroll to be brought only to the entrance of the chamber in which a parturient woman lay "that the merit of Torah may protect her," but not as a magical healing device—and by such concessions acquiesced in popular superstition. Some there were who forbade these practices altogether: "It is not enough to brand people who do this as sorcerers and conjurers; they pervert the fundamental principle of Torah in making it a healing for the body when it is intended only for a healing of the soul." But such voices did not carry far. (Trachtenberg, 105–6)

Jewish and converso readers would have referred skeptics to the sentence in the *Siete libros de la Diana* where the walls of the temple of Diana are described as being wrought in Mosaic work: "Todas las paredes eran labradas de obra Mosayca" (173/151).

With respect to the words *seven books* in the title, superstitious Jewish and converso readers would also have commented among themselves that there was a tradition in Jewish lore that the effect of a disastrous decree could be reversed by reading the decree backward (Trachtenberg, 116). According to this, the very structure of *La Diana*, in which the ills described in the first three books are reversed in the last four, would be interpreted by some zealous Jews and conversos as a reflection of Jewish superstition.

The word *seven* is twice alluded to by Sireno, with reference to

Diana's faithless cruelty, in the expression "pagar con las setenas," meaning to pay a punishment seven times greater than the offense (15/54, 270/195), or what we would call today "cruel and unusual punishment." Just as Sireno believed that he was suffering excessive punishment from Diana, many Jews and conversos would have interpreted the expression "pagar con las setenas" as their excessive punishment by Spain in the 1492 decree expelling Jews and forcing those who stayed to convert from their faith. In this sense, the suffering caused by the punishment "con las setenas" can be cured only by the seven books of chastity, *Los siete libros de la Diana*, the symbolic code for the seven books of Judaism. The main biblical reference for this interpretation would be Psalms 79, especially verse 12: "And render unto our neighbors sevenfold into their bosom their reproach wherewith they have reproached Thee, O Lord." The Jewish writer who wanted to return the reproach of his neighbors could choose no more symbolic an act than writing "seven books":

> "All sevens are beloved," says the Midrash, and we may well accept its verdict when we recall the manifold sacred associations of that numeral in Judaism. In magic the seven was second only to the three in popularity. Time and again the instructions run: repeat seven times, draw seven circles on the ground, do this daily for seven days, etc. (Trachtenberg, 119)

Of course, the number seven was a powerful symbol in Christianity as well as in other cultures, but its impact on Jewish and converso readers is what concerns us most here.

It would have surprised few Jewish and converso readers of *La Diana* that the Psalms were being subtly referred to in the text, especially because it was well known that Jorge de Montemayor, the author of *La Diana*, had published in 1558 a paraphrase of Psalm 137, "Paraphrasis en el Psalmo *Super flumina Babilonis*." In fact, one of the magical uses of the Psalms was as a cure "against compulsory baptism" (Trachtenberg, 109), and since the Psalms were often printed as a little book prohibited by the Inquisition, many Jewish and converso readers would have interpreted the book Felicia pulls from her sleeve to wake Sireno, Sylvano, and Selvagia not as the Torah, but as the Psalms. But whether it was in a book or not, the significance of this particular Psalm 137, "Super flumina Babilonis," would have eluded few Jewish and converso readers of *La Diana*.

Many Christians as well as many Jews commented on this psalm; but whatever its meaning to Christians, Psalm 137, telling about the expulsion of Jews from Jerusalem and their exile in Babylon, was a special source of hope and protest to Jews, especially to those Jews faced with expulsion from their homeland. The psalm, with only nine verses, is important enough to be recopied here.

> By the waters of Babylon, there we sat down, yea, we wept when
> we remembered Zion.
> Upon the willows in the midst thereof we hanged our harps.
> For they that led us captive asked of us word of song, and our
> tormentors asked of us mirth:
> "Sing us one of the songs of Zion." How shall we sing the Lord's
> song in a foreign land?
> If I forget thee, O Jerusalem, let my right hand forget her
> cunning.
> Let my tongue cleave to the roof of my mouth, if I remember thee
> not; if I set not Jerusalem above my chiefest joy.
> Remember, O Lord, against the children of Edom the day of
> Jerusalem; who said: "Raze it, raze it, even to the foundation
> thereof."
> O daughter of Babylon, that art to be destroyed; happy shall he be
> that repayeth thee as thou hast served us.
> Happy shall he be, that taketh and dasheth thy little ones against
> the rock.

Montemayor paraphrased Psalm 137 in a poem of 107 tercets that has been analyzed from a Christian perspective (Creel, 132–65; Rhodes, 68, 69, 104). At least one of these critics (Creel, 146) wondered whether Montemayor's poem was, in part, an attack on the Inquisition: "Is Montemayor asking for punishment of a Babylon-Inquisition, the oppressors of good Christians and the sophisticated perverters ("ingenio perverso") of the true doctrine?" But Creel did not pursue his question to a definitive answer.

Nothing in Montemayor's paraphrase of Psalm 137 can be read as exclusively Christian until lines 321–24:

> . . . and dash them against the rock of Peter.
> Blessed will they be forever, those who augment
> the holy Catholic faith on earth, and may they hold and support it
> on their shoulders. (Creel, 139)

> . . . y en la piedra de Pedro dan con ellos.
> Benditos serán siempre, los que augmentan
> la sancta fe católica en el suelo,
> y en sus hombros la tengan, y sustenten.

From a Christian perspective, the "blessed" (*benditos*) are those who, like the Inquisitors, augment—that is, exalt, fight for, and uphold—

the laws of the Catholic Church. But from a Jewish perspective, the "blessed" are the conversos, those who augment (in numbers) the Catholic faith because they are dashed by forced conversion onto the Catholic Church, the rock of Peter.

Although Creel transcribes "augmentan" (they augment), indicative mood, the rhyme clearly calls for "augmenten" (they may augment), subjunctive mood, like the other subjunctive verbs in the passage: "tengan" (they may hold), "sustenten" (they may sustain). So that translation from a Jewish perspective is full of subjunctive doubt, and should read, "and dash them against the rock of Peter. / Blessed will they [the conversos] be forever who *seem to* augment (may augment) / the holy Catholic faith on earth, / and who *seem to* hold and sustain it on their shoulders." Montemayor uses the fitly spoken word *augmenten* in precisely the way Maimonides recommended to those who were forced to pretend to convert: showing inquisitors what they want to see, but meaning also clearly what inquisitors are searching for and cannot find. Those who are convinced by his religious poetry that Montemayor was a sincere Christian, even an anti-Semite (Rhodes, 38), surely are underestimating his capacity for subtlety in an inquisitorial environment.

The poet who published in 1558, 107 subtle tercets to Psalm 137 was surely not capable of forgetting that psalm, the one that invokes dire punishment for forgetting Jerusalem, when he came to publish *La Diana* around 1559. The setting of *La Diana*, its riverbanks, its sad songs about lovers who forgot their first love, their first faith, are clearly reminiscent of Psalm 137. This melancholy setting is found in many other works, of course, but what makes *La Diana*'s a Jewish rather than simply a Renaissance melancholy (Bataillon) are the coded but clear references to exile, to parents who force their children to abandon their first love, and to the lack of free speech in Spain.

The clearest coded reference in *La Diana* to the plight of the conversos is found in Book 3. Belisa explains that she was born in a land where the inhabitants

> "are among those whom in great Spain they call Free, because of the antiquity of their houses and lineage. In this place was born the unhappy Belisa, for this is the name I took at the baptismal font where it should have pleased God I should have left my soul."

> "son de los que en la gran España llaman Libres, por el antigüedad de sus casas y linajes. En este lugar nasció la desdichada Belisa, que este nombre saqué de la pila adonde pluguiera a Dios dexara el ánima." (136/129)

The mention of free people of ancient lineage and household is a clear reference to Old Christians, that is, those whose Christianity could be traced back to the earliest times of the Reconquest, as opposed to the conversos who were called New Christians because they or their ancestors had recently been converted. Later, in Book 5, Arsileo says that Belisa is "the cause of my exile and of all the sadness that absence has made me suffer" ("la causa de mi destierro y de toda la tristeza que la ausencia me a hecho sufrir," 247/182). On the surface, Arsileo is saying that he went into exile and suffered sadness because of his love for Belisa, but, in code, Belisa is another name for Isabel, the Catholic queen who issued the decree in 1492 sending the Jews of Spain into exile. Once the code is cracked, it becomes clear why Arsileo had said moments before, "Beautiful nymph, the land where I was born has treated me in such a way that it seems that I do myself injustice in calling it mine, although on the other hand I owe it more than I would know how to overestimate" ("Hermosa nimpha, la tierra donde yo naçí me a tratado de manera que parece me hago agravio en llamarla mía, aunque por otra parte le devo más de lo que yo sabría encarecer," 247/182). It also makes more sense that Belisa would make special reference to her name and to the fact that she was named and hoped to die at the baptismal font of Roman Catholicism (136/129), a fact of which Isabela la Católica was extremely proud.

It is certainly not too far-fetched to claim that the fact that Belisa loved the father (Arsenio, 146/135), the son (Arsileo), and the unholy ghost, is a coded reference to Queen Isabela's well-known Catholic piety, especially since the text uses the words *diabolical* (*diabólico*) and *spirits* (*espíritus*) in this passage: "the diabolical Alfeo caused two spirits to take one the form of my father Arsenio and the other my form" ("el diabólico Alfeo hizo a dos espíritus que tomasse el uno la forma de mi padre Arsenio y el otro la mia," 234/176). Nor would it be far-fetched, once one perceives the code, to understand Belisa's use of the words *limpieza* (*purity*, 160/144) and, shortly after, *sangre mixturada* ("mixed blood," 159/143) to refer, not just to pure love and bloody death, but also to the laws about the purity of blood used in Isabela's Spain against Jews and conversos. Ferdinand and Isabela "issued two decrees in 1501 forbidding the children of those condemned by the tribunal [of the Inquisition] to hold any post of honor or be notaries, scriveners, physicians or surgeons. . . . With the success of the statutes it soon became necessary, when seeking public employment, to prove that one was not descended from any but Old Christians. . . . If it could be proved that an ancestor had either been made to do penance by the Inquisition or was a Moor or Jew, then his descendant was accounted of impure blood and correspondingly disabled from all public office" (Kamen, 121, 125). The tone set by the monarchs and by their government was, of course, reflective of attitudes in all segments of the population. There were dissenters among the Old Christians who tried to have the decrees rescinded, but they did not prevail until 1865, after the Inquisition itself was officially dismantled.

Another passage in Book 3 encodes clearly the severely censored environment in which the conversos were forced to express themelves, when Belisa describes at length how she and Arsileo were forced to speak in code.

> So when I saw clearly that four or five times he had committed himself to speaking and his commitment had resulted in vain because the fear he had of offending me had gotten in his way, I determined to speak to him about another topic, but not about one so far removed from his theme that he would be unable to tell me what he wanted without getting off the topic. And so I said to him: "Arsileo, are you comfortable in this country, since in the one you have been up to now, the entertainment and the conversation were probably different from our own? You must find yourself strange in it." Then he replied to me: "I do not have enough power within me, nor does my intellect have enough freedom so that I could answer that question." And changing the topic on him, in order to show him the way with opportunities, I said to him again, "They have told me that there are very beautiful shepherdesses over there, and if that is so, how ugly those of us from here must seem to you?"

> Pues viendo yo claramente que quatro o cinco vezes avía cometido el hablar y le avía salido en vano el cometimiento, porque el miedo de enojarme se le avía puesto delante, quise hablarle en otro propósito, aunque no tan lexos del suyo, que no pudiesse sin salir dél dezirme lo que desseava. Y assí le dixe:—Arsileo, ¿hallaste bien en esta tierra que, según en la que hasta agora as estado, avrá sido el entretenimiento y conversacíon diferente del nuestro?, estraño te debes hallar en ella. El entonces me respondió:—no tengo tanto poder en mí, ni tiene tanta libertad mi entendimiento que pueda responder a essa pregunta. Y mudándole el propósito, por mostralle el camino con ocasiones, le bolví a dezir:—anme dicho que ay por allá muy hermosas pastoras y si esto es assí, ¡quán mal te devemos parecer las de por acá! (156–57/141–42)

In context, of course, this passage is about the initial awkwardness some lovers encounter in speaking to each other. But, the reference to the fear of offending, and the shifting of the topic from love to conversation (free speech) in one country as compared to another, and then back again to love, is a clear signal, for those who care to use the code, that love is a topic that can be coded to express a country's affairs. Indeed, this passage is a road map for reading *La Diana*: it says that it will change itself just enough to blind inquisitors, but not so much that Jews and conversos could not read it from a perspective that favors them against the Inquisition. And when we remember that love in the text (*amor*) is coterminous with religion (*fe*), then the passage immediately following fits the code to mean that those who love enough will keep it secret, that is, those who really love their first religion will practice it in secret.

> "And if your love were so great, O Arsileo, that it gives you no room to stop loving me, keep it secret; for it is common among men of discretion such as yours to keep it [secret], even things that matter little. . . ." This my tongue said, but my eyes said something else.

> "Y si fuere tanto el amor, o Arsileo, que no te dé lugar a dexar de quererme, tenlo secreto; porque de los hombres de semejante discreción que la tuya, es tenello aun en cosas que poco importan. . . ." Esto dezía la lengua, mas otra cosa dezían los ojos. (156–57/142)

The text is so replete with images of duplicity that it would be fair for any reader, but especially for Jewish and converso readers, to conclude that where *La Diana* speaks of love, it means also something else. In particular, the verbs *disimular* (to dissemble) and *fingir* (to pretend) are used at least thirty-eight times, once in exactly the same phrase found also in *Lazarillo*: "disimulando lo mejor que pude" ("dissembling at my very best"; in *La Diana* 27/62, in *Lazarillo* 132/38).

In this setting in *La Diana* where lovers wander in exile because of their faithfulness, it cannot be accidental that parents are always the cause of disloyalty to a first love. Diana, the shepherdess, marries someone other than her first love, Sireno, in obedience to her father's wishes; Selvagia's father sends her away; Don Felix's father sends him away from Felismena; the ghost of Arsileo's father kills the ghost of its son, sending Belisa into exile from her first love. The coded message is that these parents who force disloyalty upon their children are like those Jewish parents who convert to Christianity, thus dashing their children upon the rock of Peter. Of the four principal daughters whose stories are told in *La Diana*, only those three who defied parents and remained faithful (Selvagia, Felismena, Belisa) are rewarded for their chastity with permission to enter the temple of Diana. Selvagia defied her father, and the text makes clear that she would have defied Alanio's father if necessary; Felismena defied Don Felix's father; Belisa defied her parents by leaving their home, and she defied Arsileo's father by preferring Arsileo's love to that of his father; only Diana, of these four daughters, is denied entry into the temple of chastity because she obeyed her father.

The issue of obedience to parents was by no means trivial, especially because of the commandment, "Honor thy father and thy mother." Jewish law permits the breaking of this commandment only when parents lead children to break other commandments, as for example, abjuring one's faith. Keeping the same faith is a concept repeated often in the text: to give just two significant examples, the edition of *La Diana* thought to be the oldest bears a dedication to Don Ioan Castella de Villanova, with his coat of arms that reads "With one faith, all times" ("En una fe, tos temps," *lxxxvii*); Arsileo sings about his misfortunes that "a single faith suffers it all" ("todo lo sufre una fe," 255/187).

It would not have surprised Jewish and converso readers that the philosophical underpinning for this insistence in *La Diana* on faithfulness to one love would have come from a book entitled *Dialogues of Love* and published in Italy. The author of that book, Leon Hebreo, was a member of one of the most famous Spanish Jewish families, the Abravanels, who were forced to leave Spain in 1492. In fact, Book 4, the numerical heart and thematic soul of *La Diana*, is a fitting tribute to Spain because it comprises not just the temple of Diana with Spain's Christian heroes and heroines engraved about it, but also an intellectual treatise authored by a representative member of Spain's Jews, as well as a novel, *El Abencerraje* (inserted later), about Spain's Moors.

El Abencerraje is a masterful insertion in *La Diana*, not simply because it adds appropriate Moorish content to themes about Jews and Christians, but especially because one of its most important scenes is about three knights attacking one knight. In *La Diana* also, three wild men and three knights would easily have been vanquished by Felismena alone, where others would have failed to do what she arrived on time to help them finish. The number relationships are, of necessity, slightly blurred, but the essential coded message is clear: the one God of the Jews is superior to the triune God of the Christians.

The relationships among the three religions is clearly coded according to three groups of three names: those beginning with the letter *S* (Sireno, Sylvano, Selvagia), those beginning with the letter *F*

(Felix, Felismena, Felicia), and those that should begin with the letter A (Arsenio, Arsileo, Alfeo). Although these nine names of key characters (ten, when Belisa is added to them, as I will explain) are linked deliberately, other names do not seem to be as purposefully grouped (Alanio, Amarílida, Armia, Danteo, Delio, Diana, Dórida, Duarda, Filemón, Sylvia, and so on). The S group of key names seems to represent the children of conversos who say, "yes," (sí) to Judaism; they are converted from their ill-founded love for the shepherdess Diana (Sireno and Sylvano) and Alanio/Ismenia (Selvagia), to a truth (Judaism) they had never known; these are the only characters to be touched by Felicia's book.

The F group, because it includes the sage Felicia, handmaid of the goddess of chastity, seems to represent Jews who have always been faithful (F also stands for *fe*, faith); this is clearly true of Felismena, but the text takes pains to explain the nature of Don Felix's fidelity with these words: "It is true that I loved Celia well and forgot you, but not in such a way that your worth and beauty should have passed from my memory" ("Verdad es que yo quise bien a Celia y te olvidé, mas no de manera que de la memoria se me passasse tu valor y hermosura," 298/211). Don Felix represents the kind of Jew who might wander and flirt with other gods, but does not ever really forget Judaism.

The A group represents the Moors because of its association with Felicia's opposite, the diabolic necromancer Alfeo, who is described as a traitor (235/176), and the prefix to whose name is typically Arabic (*Al*), with a suffix (*feo*) that means "ugly" in Spanish. The Christians are linked with the diabolic A group for at least two reasons: because Belisa was Alfeo's beloved and was deluded by him into believing that her lovers were dead; and also because Belisa's name should really begin with A, Abelisa, to make it a complete anagram of Isabela, the Catholic queen. According to this subtle, careful code of names, therefore, Judaism is superior to Christianity and Islam.

Although Book 4 is shaped, in its final form, so that it comprises the history of Christian Spain, the philosophy of Jewish Spain, and the courtly wars with Moorish Spain, the text that gives most meaning to *La Diana* is Psalm 137, especially as that psalm is alluded to in the final book of *La Diana*. In Book 7, after Felismena had left the palace of Felicia to wander as an armed shepherdess, she came upon a very beautiful city in Portugal that reminded her of another beautiful city in the country, presumably Spain (Vandalia being a name for Andalusia), from which she had been exiled (281/204). In exile,

Felismena sat down under a tree near the banks of a river and wept, just as the Israelites had wept in Psalm 137. When the text informs later (287/206) that the beautiful city in Portugal was Coimbra, the Jewish or converso reader would have had no difficulty understanding that the Spanish city was either Toledo, Cordoba, or even Seville, all cities that Spanish Jews over the centuries had used as metaphors for the beautiful city of Jerusalem from which all Jews, including those in Babylon in Psalm 137, had been exiled. And when the text of *La Diana* takes care to note that near this beautiful city of Coimbra was the Portuguese castle of "Monte moro vello, where virtue, ingenuity, valor, and strength remained as trophies of the deeds performed by its inhabitants at that time" ("Monte moro vello. Adonde la virtud, el ingenio, valor y esfuerço avían quedado por tropheos de las hazañas que los habitadores dél, en aquel tiempo avían hecho," 287/207), most Jewish and converso readers would have recognized a reference to the legend of Montemayor.

According to this legend, the town of Montemayor was under siege by the Moors in the ninth century, and when its abbott realized that the town could not survive the siege, he ordered that all the inhabitants be slain or thrown from the town walls rather than surrender to the Moors (Creel, 45; Menéndez Pidal). Just like other Jewish and converso writers before and after him had done (Diego de San Pedro, Fernando de Rojas, the anonymous author of *Lazarillo*, Cervantes), Jorge de Montemayor inserts his name into his work with maximum artistic symbolism. For the writer Jorge de Montemayor, the town Montemayor had the same symbolic value that Numancia had for Cervantes: it was a metaphor for Masada, the rock fortress where hundreds of Jews slew themselves rather than surrender to the Romans. The allusion is, once again, to Psalm 137 and to the dashing of little children against the rock. The coded message is that if the Christians of the town of Montemayor could dash their children against the rocks rather than surrender to infidels, then, surely the Jews, instead of dashing their children against the rock of Peter by baptizing them into the Catholic Church, should remember their own rock, Masada, where Jews slew their children rather than surrender them to the Romans. In other words, the main theme of *La Diana* has come full circle: "antes muerta que mudada," "better dead than changed," better suicide than conversion. These words, which Sireno said he had seen Diana write with her fingers in the sand as she was seated at a riverbank, also confirm that the major spiritual source for *La Diana* is Psalm 137, and that Diana's major sin for which she is denied entry into the Temple of Chastity is not simply that she had forgotten Sireno but that she had broken her vow to remember Jeru-salem: "Seated upon the sand / of that river I saw her / where with her finger she wrote: / 'better dead than changed'" ("Sobre el arena sentada / de aquel río la vi yo / do, con el dedo escrivió: / antes muerta que mudada," 53/14).

CHAPTER 8

Life as a Text
We Learn to Read: Exit

for Berel Lang

Even under the burden of massacre, life seems bound to discourse—to rehearsal, to recollection and reflection, and then, too, beyond its own impulses, to answering questions asked by a new generation searching for its own voice.
BEREL LANG, *Act and Idea in the Nazi Genocide,* 229

THE LAST time I read the *Lazarillo,* I cried. For all the insults I had done to it, for all the insensitivities of my friends and colleagues, I wept. And now I know that whenever I visit with that text again, the pleasure it will bring me will be deeper, a pleasure always at the brink of its own final solution, a pleasure always mixed with tears and catastrophic tragedy, the kind of marginal pleasure that leads, sometimes unwittingly, to the discovery of whole new worlds of seeing, and to the destruction and reconstruction of Old World ways of reading.

Reading properly is the key to understanding any text, but reading texts like *Lazarillo* properly is vital, because the lives of real people are at stake in the meaning of the text contemporary with its composition, and because the major significance of the text of *Lazarillo* after its composition is about how all readers choose to approach it, that is, about how all readers live. As Alan Deyermond put it in the first and last sentences that frame his masterly little book about *Lazarillo,* "De te fabula narratur—the story is about you. . . . The story, in short, is about us" (1975, 9, 98). And so it made me sad, as well, to read the opinion of a bright young leader of the next generation of Hispanists that "the story [*Lazarillo*] is not 'about' us . . . as Deyermond claims" (Paul Julian Smith, 98). The world can ill afford to have yet another generation misread texts like *Lazarillo*.

What does *Lazarillo* tell us exactly about ourselves? Up to 1975, the most reliable typology of *Lazarillo* readers is Deyermond's. Deyermond shows that some of us are trusting while others are skeptical, and the skeptics (those who do not believe Lazaro) tend to consider the trusting readers to be gullible. Some of us are so pious that we cannot conceive of people who would poke fun at things they adore; others are so irreligious that we see godlessness in every delightful joke. Some of us are so unimaginatively in love with realism that we think that art can only portray what the artist can see with real eyes, not with the mind's eye; others are so given to fantasy that we see symbolism in every commonplace. Some of us are so elitist that we recognize as art only the learned "classical" allusions; others among us are so deluded by the masses that we see art in every piece of vulgar folklore.

After Deyermond (1975), three other recent typologies come to mind. Gordon Minter suggests (1987), after Rafael Sánchez-Ferlosio, that we are either like those who section the onions of life in order to get at a core, or we are like those who shuck the cloves of garlic in life, respecting the integrity of each grain. If we are onionlike, we hanker after artistic unity in *Lazarillo*; we want all seven *tratados* to make a neat, logically artistic whole; if we are garlicsome, we are comfortable with seven independent artistic *tratados* free-floating in a search for survival of the fittest in an artistic whole. For Peter Dunn (1989), we are conditioned either to keep trying "to fill all the gaps," to keep searching for inaccessible answers to an ever-extending list of unnecessary questions, or we are wise enough to accept that some things in life are inherently permeable. To try to fill in all the gaps is to believe that we are capable of reading *Lazarillo* as His Grace, for example, might have read it; to accept the text as permeable is to realize that we have, over time, acquired different, more permeable tools for reading texts like *Lazarillo*, that we can stay loose and accept the fact that not all questions need to be asked and answered.

For Paul Julian Smith (1988), we tend to be positivistic humanist pictorialists severed unaesthetically, like handleless prehistoric axes, from the reality we seek to understand; instead, we should be like wild Derridean tulips framing the gilded Kantian margins of the (Cézanne) masterpieces we transcend. The general reader will forgive the postmodern jargon, but Smith seems to be saying that to understand *Lazarillo* we should see that subjectivity is what makes the text, like Derrida's *parergon*, marginal. The Greek word *ergon* refers to the work itself, while the *parergon* is the essential ancillary made for the work, like the frame made especially for the painting; so that for Smith subjectivity is the frame (*parergon*) around *Lazarillo,* "the apparently secondary and subordinate term which is in fact essential to the operation" and understanding of *Lazarillo* (85). Smith also interprets that identity in the text moves from what Lacan calls a "specular" (mirror image) stage to an imaginary stage, as Lazarillo the child stops seeing himself reflected in the world around him and becomes Lazaro the man, capable of imagining or re-creating the world around him as well as enticing readers to reconstruct the world that he has imagined.

I have no quarrel whatever with any of these types of reading. And yet, because none of them quite comfortably accommodates the way I read, I feel I should propose, without seeking to impose it on any other reader, a typology of my own. It seems to me that categories of readers do not arrange themselves in neat hierarchies or convenient on-the-one-hand-on-the-other oppositions. The only criterion I would propose for reading all texts is intersubjectivity, because each text invites its peculiar optimum form of reading, and only intersubjectivity can inform the reader about what that optimum approach should be.

For *Lazarillo,* it seems to me, readers fall along a wide spectrum ranging from those who seek to bully or torture the text like inquisitors hankering after the facts, to those who enter the text with intersubjective respect; many points along the spectrum might at once be reflected in the same reader. Three types of readers move along this spectrum: those who let the text speak for the author, that is, for the creator of Lazaro; those who let the text speak for Lazaro, who purports to be its author; and those who let the text speak for itself. Again, countless variations of these three ways of reading can be found in a single reader.

The most serious impediment to valid reading is permeability. This is represented in all the types of reading typified by Deyermond, Minter, Dunn, and Smith: the calls for trust in a reliable narrator, for a garlic approach, for an end to interminable lists, for a wild-tulip *parergon* approach, all reflect fear of permeable disorder. These approaches all claim to liberate the text from an oppressive, insatiable reader; in fact, they all seem to want to imprison the text in differently framed forms of *parerga,* hiding it away securely from further investigation, legitimate as well as harrassing. Fear of permeability is very similar to the fear of circularity discussed in my opening chapter. Permeable arguments are perceived to have holes in their logic; logic, especially Aristotelian logic, is deemed desirable because it is believed to be impermeable to counterclaims. "Mutually permeable" arguments are held to be worst of all, I suppose, because their logic has holes both ways, through and through, thoroughly pervious.

But then there are artists, like converso artists, who take permeability and make beautiful filigree out of it, so that it becomes logical for the same beautiful object to contain opposite meanings through the same apertures that to some eyes seem like undesirable permeability. These artists teach us that permeability is an issue only when the text is being asked to speak either for its author or, in the case of *Lazarillo*, for Lazaro himself who claims to be an author. As long as the text is whole, free from obvious lacunae and editorial intervention, as long as the text is not a fragment, permeability cannot be an issue if the text is engaged intersubjectively and made to speak for itself. As long as the text is whole, there will be no unfillable gaps in its meaning, and when engaged intersubjectively its significance will never be static, as text and reader continue to grow through time. Through time, the text continues to exist in the memory of the intersubjective reader not as an object consumed but, to the extent possible, as an equal subject with the appropriate respect that text demands. This appropriately respected text in the reader's memory permits the intersubjective reader to be constantly prepared to pre-read the text whenever the reader encounters information outside the text but relevant to a full understanding of it.

Pre-reading, that is, thinking about a text before engaging it intersubjectively, is so crucial to excellent criticism and, simultaneously, so difficult to learn to do well, that it is instructive to examine how we relate to and store texts in our memories. The "conversations" that take place between a reader and that reader's memory of the text are subjective (not yet intersubjective) dramatizations in which the reader speaks for the reader and also attempts to speak for the text by impersonating it, imagining, as faithfully as possible, what the text would say to the reader if it were to speak for itself. As the "conversation" takes place, there is, strictly speaking, only one subject present, namely, the reader—including, of course, the memory of the text im-personated in that reader. The printed text is somewhere else, on a bookshelf or on the desk or couch next to the reader. The location of the text and its written (hard-copy) format are not what make this "conversation" subjective, because if the reader were an ancient epic bard or a tribal historian or a modern actor or the kind of Jew who knows (stores) the entire Torah by heart (just in case times turn inquisitorial and Torahs are burned), then it is conceivable that the reader would be carrying the entire text accurately within memory; what makes the "conversation" subjective is the fact that, in order to prepare appropriately for an encounter with the text, the reader chooses to impersonate the text instead of letting it speak for itself. Similar preparations occur normally in life: on our way to an important meeting, we often rehearse scenarios in an effort to make the encounter more meaningful; we say to ourselves, for example, "If I say this, then they will say this, but then I can always reply with this," and so on. These conversations are similar to what Gadamer (236) called "fore-projects," and they are important exercises because they provide the reader with an appropriate opportunity to approach all texts, especially works like converso texts, with appropriate respect, the respect they demand if they are to yield interpretations capable of enriching the experience of most readers.

There is nothing novel about pre-reading; many readers proceed in similar ways. What is novel, I think, is the suggestion that more significant understanding will be achieved if subjectivity is infused at its very roots with as much intersubjective respect for the memory of the text as is possible even at the stage of pre-reading. The ego is a better-prepared recipient of understanding when it injects into itself as much of the other as is appropriate. The well-prepared hermeneutically trained critic is not a detective on the prowl for felons; the well-prepared critic is a subject inviting a like and (when all samenesses and differences are reconciled) ultimately equal subject to a mutually enriching encounter. Proper preparation for the encounter is essential if the text is to be made to reveal its current newness:

> Rather, a person trying to understand a text is *prepared* for it to say something. That is why a hermeneutically trained mind must be, *from the start*, sensitive to the text's quality of newness. But this kind of sensitivity involves neither "neutrality" in the matter of the object nor the extinction of one's self, but the conscious assimilation of one's own fore-meanings and prejudices. The important thing is to be aware of one's own bias, so that the text may present itself in all its newness and thus be able to assert its own truth against one's own fore-meanings. (emphasis added, Gadamer, 238)

Just as it made me sad to read these converso texts this time around, it also saddened me to read in Paul Julian Smith's otherwise brilliant book that "literary theory in Spanish begins later than elsewhere and is, initially at least, overwhelmingly dependent on Latin and Italian antecedents" (p. 19). This claim is made one page after the writer had stated with consonantal blindness that "Covarrubias advises the prospective artist or writer to polish a work (*limar*) and to lick it (*lamer*), just as the mother-bear licks its formless young into shape" (p. 18). Smith does not see that *limar* and *lamer* should mean the same, in Covarrubias' theoretical opinion, because of the consonantal stem pattern *lmr;* Smith misses the essential point that Spanish literary theory does not begin with Covarrubias and is *not* "overwhelmingly dependent," as he claims, "on Latin and Italian antecedents." Literary theory in Spain, not always dependent on European sources written in Latin and Italian, goes all the way back to the ninth century, as far as we can now tell, and was often written in Hebrew and Arabic as well as Latin. Spain can only be on the margin of literary theory if by "margin" one means not late or backward but at the very least equal and different, if not ahead of the rest of Europe. Eurocentric standards of measurement will not suffice.

Spain is, in (literary) Europe, a marginal country. Spain is a converso country. Spain created converso Moors with the final defeat of the Moors in 1492, accelerating the centuries-long enervation of Spain's Moorish (human) resources. With the persecution of the Jews in 1391 and their expulsion in 1492, Spain converts itself from being the center of the Jewish world and the marginal diabolical backwater of Christianity, in the opinion of most Europeans who wrote about it, to being the (envied, often hated) center of the Christian world. Spain is the converso country that has given birth to an entire continent full of conversos, including mestizos and other myriad denominations of hyphenated human beings. It is essential that we understand, now, what happened in Spain so that we do not lose, again, the opportunity for multicultural tolerance and enrichment. There is no inquisition now in America; there is, however, an excess of multicultural ignorance. If we understand, now, what theories Spain transported to America and how, we stand a better chance of knowing ourselves and understanding others.

To get at the essence of Spanish literary theory of the Golden Age, Paul Julian Smith finds it helpful (and indeed it is) to use a sonnet by Quevedo. Quevedo represents the best of Spain's excess. For essence, few, in my opinion, will take us closer to Spain than Góngora. Is there anywhere a better title for all of Spain than *Soledades* (*Solitudes*)? Does anyone understand better than Góngora what it is like for a powerful country (or, better, for a country that seems like a powerful giant) to look at the entire known world like *Polyphemos*, with both its precious eyes dug out and replaced by one unnatural eye in the middle of its forehead? Do any of Quevedo's sonnets speak for Spain as does this one by Góngora?

A CÓRDOBA

¡Oh excelso muro, oh torres coronadas
de honor, de majestad, de gallardía!
¡Oh gran río, gran rey de Andalucía,
de arenas nobles, ya que no doradas!
¡Oh fértil llano, oh sierras levantadas,
que privilegia el cielo y dora el día!
¡Oh siempre gloriosa patria mía,
tanto por plumas cuanto por espadas!
¡Si entre aquellas ruinas y despojos
que enriquece Genil y Darro baña
tu memoria no fue alimento mío,
nunca merezcan mis ausentes ojos
ver tu muro, tus torres y tu río,
tu llano y sierra, oh patria, oh flor de España!

Oh wall sublime, Oh towers crowned
with honor, majesty, and gallantry!
Oh great river, great king of Andalusia,
with noble, though not gilded sands!
Oh fertile plain, oh elevated mountains,
that heaven adorns [at night] and daylight gilds!
Oh ever glorious motherland of mine,
as much for its pens as for its swords!
If among those ruins and spoils
that [the river] Genil enriches and Darro bathes,
the memory of you was not my nourishment,
never may my absent eyes deserve
to see your wall, your towers and your river,
your plain and mountain range, oh motherland, oh flower of Spain!

The poem has been analyzed too many times for me to repeat here what many critics have said, except to add what I have been telling students for the last twenty years or so: this sonnet's essence is revealed if it is read as a gloss on Psalm 137 (the same psalm, by the way, that Montemayor glossed), especially verses 5, 6: "If I forget thee, O Jerusalem, let my right hand forget her cunning. If I do not remember thee, let my tongue cleave to the roof of my mouth, if I prefer not Jerusalem above my chiefest joy." Góngora's knowledge of this psalm is the matter of an entire book I will never have the time to write. Suffice it here to say that the poet feels his eyes ought to be plucked out if he ever forgets Córdoba, the Spanish city that was known for centuries as the New Jerusalem.

But the lyric voice in this and many other poems cannot be assigned to the poet, in this case Góngora, alone: the lyric voice, the essence of this poem, is meant to belong to anyone reading the poem. So that if the poem is read by the monarch responsible for Spain, for example, the poem's meaning instantly amplifies itself; if the poem is read by Spain itself, personified, then it begins to mean that Spain deserves to have its eyes plucked out, not simply temporarily absent but permanently removed, if it were to neglect its Córdoba, its Mecca and Medina, its New Jerusalem. No wonder that, in Góngora's text, Spain lost its precious eyes, its Moors and Jews, and made itself unnaturally blind, half-blind at best, or, better, two-thirds blind with one unnatural eye in the middle of its monocultural forehead.

And if it is read by one of us today, by someone seeking to understand Spain's literary theory and heritage, for example, then the poem's essential significance, not just its obvious rhetorical excess, should be equally clear. Spain, we see, had two literary Golden Ages at least, if not three: the one that is usually spoken of today by Hispanists, the Age of Cervantes and Góngora and Quevedo; an earlier one most Jews today still refer to as the Golden Age of Hebrew literature, the Spain in which literary theorists like Maimonides were born and Moses Ibn Ezra, Ibn Gabirol, and Yehudah Halevi wrote their poems; and a third one concurrent with the Jewish Golden Age that made Spain a kind of Medina for many Moslems and gave rise to literary genius like that of Averroës. Maimonides, of course, as Leo Strauss explains, makes ample use of Arabic literary theory and practice.

Quevedo and Góngora are two of the world's greatest poets. Francisco Gómez de Quevedo y Villegas (1580–1645) was perhaps the bitterest enemy of Luis de Góngora y Argote (1561–1627). Quevedo was proud of being an Old Christian, unreachable by the arm of the Spanish Inquisition because his bloodline showed no trace of Jewish or Moorish ancestry. Knowing well that it could cost Góngora his life, Quevedo accused Góngora in a published sonnet of being of Jewish descent: "I will grease my verses with pork fat / so that you do not sink your teeth in them for me, Gongorilla" ("Yo untaré mis versos con tocino / porque no me los muerdas, Gongorilla"). When Góngora's major works appeared, Quevedo attempted to ridicule them by calling them "highfalutin Latinspeak" ("culta latiniparla"). Quevedo understood very well that Góngora was forced to invent a tortured form of language in order to avoid persecution; what must have irritated Quevedo was that he could not crack Góngora's secret code. So Quevedo lashed back at Góngora in material ways, since poetic ways were not effective enough at destroying him. When Góngora was sixty-four years old and in financial straits, Quevedo bought the house Góngora was living in, forcing him to move (Alborg, 522–23). The two hated each other, and their hatred teaches us an important lesson about favored and oppressed human beings in times of persecution. Future generations of Hispanists and general readers should not select Quevedo blindly and ignore what Góngora was fighting.

What Old Christians like Quevedo do for Góngora is drive him more reconditely closer to essence. By that I mean that Quevedo demonstrates to Góngora that he, Quevedo, can get dangerously close to exposing Góngora's essential meaning, which means, of course, for Góngora, certain death. So Góngora becomes, like Salman Rushdie, forced to find more subtle, more essentially artistic ways to express himself. As Maimonides might have put it, Quevedo forces Góngora to make his silver filigree less transpicuous and his golden apple less accessible—in the memorable opening words of Góngora's famous poem, *Solitudes*, "Pasos de un peregrino son errante [A Córdoba]," footsteps of a wandering Jew yearning for Jerusalem.

By the same reading, Ovid in Góngora's *Polifemo* is pure camouflage, transpicuous filigree intended to keep the inquisitor's eyes away from Homer's *Odyssey*, so that intelligent readers like Robert Jammes would write, "Mais il est clair qu'une reconstitution archéologique des aventures d'Ulysse ne l'intéressait guère" ("but it is clear that an archeological reconstruction of the adventures of Ulysses hardly interested him [Góngora] at all," 562). But a glimpse of the golden apple can be seen in the title Juan López de Vicuña, the first editor of Góngora's poems, chose for the complete works of Góngora: López de Vicuña does not refer to Ovid (Quevedo, the same Old Christian Quevedo who wrote the infamous sonnet "To a Nose," would have said here not Ovid but Nasón, Supernose; when Quevedo wrote "las doce tribus de narices era," "the twelve tribes of nose it was," he meant to drive people into the prisons of the Spanish Inquisition), but to Homer—*Obras en verso del Homero español* (*Works in Verse from the Spanish Homer*). Because the inquisitive hunters think they have the source (Ovid), they neglect to inquire after the full meaning and significance of the title *Polifemo* in Spain from the year 1391 on, especially to the time that Góngora was writing and after. In like manner, the Italian setting and the use of Italian texts (Stigliani, Marino) in *Polifemo* are pure Maimonidean filigree to divert eyes away from Spain.

Góngora has people like Quevedo in mind in the only written defense we have of his style, after he had been ridiculed for turgidity.

He writes in response to an attack on his style published in an anonymous "Letter from a Friend":

> I do not send the *Solitudes* out [into the reading world] confused, but malice in the will [of others] attributes confusion in their own language to the party infected with their malice. To [the remark about] the grace of Pentecost, I would like to refrain from responding [but also obviate the response, in the sense of parry the blow], because I do not want you, Sir, so much an aficionado of the things of the Old Testament.

> Yo no envío confusas las *Soledades,* sino las malicias de las voluntades en su mismo lenguaje hallan confusión por parte del sujeto inficionado con ellas. "A la gracia de Pentecostés querría obviar el responder, que no quiero a V.M. tan aficionado a las cosas del Testamento Viejo. (Góngora 1987, 173)

Góngora comes dangerously close to revealing himself here; he is angry, not just witty; he is not simply playing with the words *aficionado* (amateur) and *inficionado* (infected) as some readers would think (note the consonant patterns and the play on vowels). First he demonstrates that his attacker does not understand the Old Testament story of the Tower of Babel; then he begins to show, but stops abruptly because of the danger, that the attacker does not know what the Christian understanding of Pentecost has to do with the Old Testament, namely, that for Jews what Christians call Pentecost is Shabuoth, the celebration of the fiftieth day after Passover and, more important, the celebration of the giving of the law to Moses. His attacker might think that Góngora does not want him to be "an aficionado of the Old Testament" because that would mean that his attacker is converso and subject to the scrutiny of the Inquisition; but Góngora also means that he does not want his attacker looking too closely at the Old Testament because then he would be able to understand Góngora's work better and expose Góngora to the Inquisition. For "malicias" in Góngora's response, knowledgeable Jewish and converso readers will understand "slander"; for "inficionado," they will know to read "infected with leprosy." There is no better converso text than Góngora's angry response to the person who viciously and ignorantly attacked his work in that anonymous "Letter from a Friend" ("Carta de un amigo").

Some critics might object that it is not possible to impose a meaning on Polyphemos in Góngora's work that does not also apply to other writers who use the theme. The immediate reply to this objection is as follows: show me a poet who uses Polyphemos and also writes a poem like "A Córdoba," and also writes a poem like "Soledades" in which a pilgrim ("peregrino") wanders through a Mosaic (Musa or Muça is the Arabic name for Moses) wilderness, and I will say the same thing about that poet that I have said about Góngora.

Perhaps it is too late for Hispanists of my generation to see in the works of Góngora and Quevedo a lesson to the entire world about the necessity for multicultural rather than monocultural approaches to literature and to life. This is why it is so important, in my opinion, to speak directly to bright young critics like Paul Julian Smith, to tell them not to apply the works of critics like Derrida and Freud and Marx blindly, without really seeing them for what they are essentially. Derrida, Marx, and Freud, as Susan Handelman has demonstrated in her *Slayers of Moses*, are not part of a monocultural (Christian) European tradition, but part of a tradition rooted also in Judaism, in a Judaic attitude toward texts that was, at a crucial point in its development, infused with Islamic modes of thought. About Spain, an entire book entitled *Writing in the Margin* should not be published in 1988 with only passing reference to Américo Castro, if only out of respect for his *Españoles al margen!* Smith makes reverential excuses for his exclusion of women; he also excludes Moors and Jews, something a deeper reading of Américo Castro would not have let him do. To forget Moors and Jews in Spain, as Góngora (not Quevedo) reminds us, is to deserve blindness, that is, to need a blind man's guide, a *lazarillo*. Another generation of readers and critics should not remain blind to the full multicultural value of Spanish literature.

The next generation of readers and critics, it seems to me, is not well served by the existing editions of many of Spain's literary masterpieces. I have worked with a number of editions of these three converso texts before me. It has been a frustrating task, because none of these editions pays intersubjective respect to textual theory and practice in Spain. No country preserved, produced, edited, and transmitted texts with any greater love than Spain. And yet the philological criteria used by most Hispanists continue to be classical. A few philologists, like Margherita Morreale, for example, are as knowledgeable of sacred texts (including the Koran) as they are of other texts, but their practice seems to be, as far as I can tell, not influenced by what they know about holy books in Spain. Since I cannot teach myself in this lifetime what I need to know about editing, I wait, with *Lazarillo, Abencerraje*, and *La Diana*, for better editions of Spain's precious literary works. Unfortunately, no country burned books with any greater zeal than Spain, and so my wait might well be all in vain.

What do I want from these textual critics ?

○ When they edit medieval and Golden Age Spanish texts, especially converso texts, I want no easy assumptions like this one: "The Lachmannian method, as is well known, is quite safe in optimum conditions—and the *Lazarillo* almost assembles those conditions together ("el método lachmaniano que, como es sabido, en condiciones óptimas—y el *Lazarillo* casi las reúne—es bastante seguro," Blecua, 1974, 49). Did Lachmann understand why a converso text would have to be floated in manuscript form to test how exposed it was to being fully understood? Did he understand what would cause a converso text to be altered, even after it was published? Karl Lachmann (1793–1851) was a great philologist who thought he knew how to read between Homer's lines. Lachmann's findings are no longer widely accepted, but his methods, strangely enough, are still predominant in European philology.

○ I need more information on the transmission of converso texts, more variant readings, less punctuation, and fewer of the editor's opinions about an optimum *Ur*-text.

○ I want books like Frederick J. Norton's *Printing in Spain, 1501–1520* to give due consideration to printers of Spanish books outside of Spain during the same period. I want them to tell me, for example, how many of Quevedo's books were printed in Antwerp and by whom. I want more biographical information on the printers, especially printers of Spanish books outside of Spain.

○ Most of all, I would like the critical apparatus to pay special attention to words and references that are of cross-cultural importance, with a glossary of those words, perhaps, at the end of the text; words such as *confesso, musa, peregrino, Córdoba, Numancia, odyssey, Pentecost, lázaro, malicias* cannot be assumed to have monocultural meanings and significance in all texts. In brief, I do not want an edition that is completely blind to the existence of converso and *morisco* cultures in Spain, especially from 1391 on.

It sounds simple enough, but it means, in fact, that new editions are sorely needed not just for the three texts studied here, but for the works of many major writers, Góngora and Cervantes among them. Let us take a moment, exiting, to begin to illustrate the need

by looking at the often explicated opening lines of the second stanza
of Góngora's *Polifemo* to see what else we see:

Templado, pula en la maestra mano
el generoso pájaro su pluma.

Trained, on the hand of its master,
let the noble falcon preen its feathers.

In the hands of one of the world's greatest poets, every letter counts
for music, the famous "musicality of the *Polifemo*" (Colin Smith). Look
at the architecture of the consonants, the placement of the cluster
pl/pr in tem*pl*ado, *pu*la, *pá*jaro, *pl*uma; look at the use of *m*. Then
look at the vowels, the internal assonantal rhymes in *a-o*: templ*a*d*o*,
m*a*n*o*, p*á*jar*o*, and in *u-a*: p*u*l*a*, pl*u*m*a*. All of this has been said
before, since 1927, at least, when contemporary Spanish poets and
scholars like Dámaso Alonso, remembering one of Spain's Golden
Ages and the tricentenary of Góngora's death, began to study him
again in earnest. What has not been said before, as far as I know, is
that it was easier, much easier for Góngora to play with consonants
and vowels than it was for an Old Christian poet, like Quevedo, for
example; Góngora must have been accustomed to reading the Old
Testament in the original Hebrew, with and without vowel markers,
like Fray Luis de León, who was jailed for five years by the Spanish
Inquisition for doing it. Góngora's music, tortured out of the violent
hyperbaton for which he was attacked, is doleful, like the blues, a
strange new song: "For there our captors required of us songs, and
our tormentors mirth, saying, 'Sing us one of the songs of Zion!' How
shall we sing the Lord's song in a strange land?" (Psalm 137:3–4).
Quevedo's music cannot be favorably compared with Góngora's. Quevedo is the master of cacophonous excess, not music: just listen to
his sonnet "La vida empieza en lágrimas y caca" ("Life begins in tears
and shit").

To illustrate the lesson further, let me use another example from
my own life's experience. A few years ago, I wrote an article about
mestureros (meddlers, or better, slanderers), an important word in
medieval Spanish literature. I tried to show a direct relationship between this word and a Hebrew word for leper, *metzorah*, the name
for an entire portion of Torah, Leviticus 14:1–15:33. For years I could
not understand why the Christian experts who read the article rejected it unanimously on the same grounds: they found the etymological arguments lexically and linguistically flawed. The Jewish experts
who read the article, on the other hand, thought it important; one

of them threatened to take the article from me and publish it under his own name when I told him that I did not really care if it was published or not. I noted the division between Christian and Jewish readers of the same piece, but I did not really understand the difference until I realized that it was easy for the Jewish readers, because they had training in Hebrew philology as well as in European philology, to accept wordplay based on consonantal stem patterns, a concept harder for philologists trained only in European linguistics to penetrate. The distinction was not between Jewish and Christian, as it seemed at first, but rather between monocultural and multicultural philologists. Many Jews do not know Hebrew; some Christians do. Editors of converso texts should be aware that, in Spain, European philology will not always suffice.

One might think these demands of textual critics too harsh. In fact, earlier editions like those by Francisco López Estrada (1962) of *La Diana* did pay more respect to the history of the text, and Alberto Blecua (1972, 179–85) does give variant readings of *Lazarillo*. But recently there has been a tendency for editors to take too much license on the misguided premise that twentieth-century scholarship and textual methods are indubitably and always superior to scholarship and methods contemporary with the text. In brief, twentieth-century editors tend to approach medieval and sixteenth-century texts like conquerors, when texts like converso masterpieces will not yield fully to any approach but intersubjective respect.

To presume to change any part of any masterpiece is folly, if one understands by masterpiece a work whose elements are so assembled that to alter any part of it is to destroy it. In a work like *Lazarillo*, for example, to put a single accent mark on the word *confesso* is to drastically alter the artistry of the text. Converso writers were prepared to do violence to a language that belongs to a culture that would certainly do violence to the writer whose full protesting meaning is discovered. Góngora, for example, twisted Spanish words out of their normal word order, so as to wring music out of the malicious persecution of the Tower of Babel, and blind what was a one-eyed Babylon for him: the Spanish Inquisition.

Thus we see that, in inquisitorial Spain, texts and life are intricately interwoven by master weavers, but not always in the monocultural ways to which most of us are accustomed, and we must learn to read the different warp, the peculiar cross-cultural woof. Received and ancient texts become unusual metaphors for everyday life: Homer's *Odyssey* becomes a metaphor for the wandering Jewish people; the legend of Odysseus and Polyphemos becomes a metaphor for

David (Jews and conversos) and Goliath (the Spanish Inquisition); the story of Perets in Genesis becomes a metaphor for the absurd lineages forced upon Jews and conversos by the statutes regulating purity of blood; Psalm 137 becomes a weary song of exile from Spain; John 1:20 becomes a metaphoric code for the word *converso*; the parable of the sower becomes a metaphor for deep and superficial readers; the legend of the Judgment of Paris becomes a metaphor for the debates among the three religions—Judaism, Christianity, and Islam—learned, sometimes well, often unrecognizably, from Jews; the legends of Numantia (in a lesser known play by Cervantes) and Montemayor become metaphors for Masada; the proverbial sayings of Celestina and Sancho Panza, wisdom of the common people, become metaphoric links between love and religion, between everyday life and sacred texts. To crack the code, the reader must be at home with constantly shifting perspectives, filigree techniques of blindness and insight, just as Jorge de Montemayor described in his map for reading *La Diana*. But once revealed, each clue to the code must be as clear as the golden apple transfixed transpicuously behind the proverbial filigree of Maimonides. Each clue must be rooted visibly in the text.

If I had time enough (and a small army of graduate students), I would design a hermeneutical project for revisiting certain portions of the corpus of works written in Spanish, from immediately after the slaughter and conversion of Jews throughout Spain in 1391 up to the death of Góngora in 1627. There is an unusual story to be told about how expression in the Spanish language is mutated from the prosaic occasional *cancionero* poetry of Alfonso de Baena and Francisco Imperial, through the maze of labyrinthine allusions of the poet Juan de Mena and the polyvalent ambiguities of Cervantes, to the hermetic pellucid opacities of Góngora.

It is a story that might chart the vital ontological need for subtlety, a word known in theory and practice by late fourteenth-century poets like Baena and Imperial. This subtlety becomes, in the hands of fifteenth-century poets like Juan de Mena, a verbal maze that deliberately distorts the Spanish language in its Latin roots with what Quevedo ridiculed as "highfalutin Latinspeak." In the sixteenth and seventeenth centuries, subtlety becomes an ingeniously insane linguistic necessity for coded safety, as in Cervantes' "ingenioso hidalgo" (ingenious [also mad] gentleman) and Góngora's letter written, in response to a "letter more audacious than ingenious" ("carta, más que ingeniosa, atrevida"), to explain that his *Solitudes* "has the useful function of bringing the witty engine [the brain, *ingenio*] to life" ("tiene utilidad avivar el ingenio"). This story about subtlety is a story about what creativity can do to persecution in an inquisitorial environment. It is a story that would not exclude Spain's empire overseas—for example, Góngora's hyphenated New World relative, Carlos de Sigüenza y Góngora, who invented (in an underrated book entitled *The Misfortunes of Alonso Ramirez*) another *Lazarillo* and made him wander not through Europe but through Central America, the New World islands and the Philippines.

But since I cannot write the full story of all the texts that defied the Inquisition in Spain, I have limited myself to three of those texts only, in order that I might pass more rapidly to how the story was continued in the world called new by Spain, to how the story lives today in America. America does not now divide itself into Old Christians and New Christians called conversos, as Spain once did, but, as I suggest in the preface of this book, the story of converso writers in sixteenth-century Spain is not without application today. My next book, which I call *Healing the Hyphenated Hemisphere*, begins with the following two paragraphs.

America is more fully representative of hyphenated human beings than any other place on earth. In North America, there are French-Canadians, English-Canadians, Native-Canadians, Italian-, Irish-, Polish-, German-, and every other kind of European-Americans, Jewish-Americans, African-Americans, Asian-Americans, Hispanic-Americans (some of whom prefer to be called Latinos), and so on. In Central America and South America, there are mestizos in so many variegated mixtures of European, Indian, and African that administrators have had to stop keeping track of the categories Spain once catalogued with scrutiny. And in the New World islands, all races have intermingled to make beautiful hyphenated human beings.

It is, of course, a geographical coincidence that all these hyphenated human beings live in a hemisphere whose northern and southern continents are separated by a Central American hyphen that has, in the twentieth century, been severed at the isthmus of Panama. But how these hyphenated human beings have come to be what they are is certainly no coincidence. Four world powers are principally responsible for the phenomenon of hyphenation that is America: Iberia (that is, Spain and Portugal), England, France, and the United States. From the arrival of Columbus in 1492 until the United States defeated Spain in the Spanish American War in 1898, Spain maintained considerable control in some part of Central and South America and the islands.

Now, as I type that sentence from my next book, I think for the first time, "1492 to 1898! The Spanish Inquisition was dismantled in

1834! What were the effects of an inquisitorial environment that lasted officially in the New World from 1492 to 1834? Did New World writers also resist hyphenation in ways as heroically creative as those invented by converso writers in Spain? In the New World, Spain's lesson speaks to us even today. For hundreds of years since 1492, Spain's monocultural inquisitorial laws have dictated the shape of development in the New World. Can those laws—which permitted the involuntary removal of millions of human beings from Africa and Asia, forcing them to sing new songs in a strange land, mixing the three continents of the Old World irreversibly in the New—ever be rescinded?"

On 31 March 1992—in a ceremony attended also by the President of Israel, Chaim Herzog—King Juan Carlos of Spain rescinded the edict of expulsion of the Jews of Spain issued by the Catholic kings five hundred years earlier, to the day, in 1492. It took five hundred years to rescind a text that took thousands of lives. But there were those who defied that text by creating other much more beautiful immortal texts that will enrich our lives and the lives of a million other readers, forever and ever.

BIBLIOGRAPHY

The Texts in Spanish

Abencerraje. 1980. Francisco López Estrada, ed. Madrid: Cátedra.
La vida de Lazarillo de Tormes y de sus fortunas y adversidades. 1972. Alberto Blecua, ed. Madrid: Clásicos Castalia.
Montemayor, Jorge de. 1962. *Los siete libros de la Diana*. Francisco López Estrada, ed. Madrid: Clásicos Castellanos.

The Texts in English

The Abencerraje and the Beautiful Jarifa. 1964. John E. Keller, trans., and Francisco López Estrada, ed. Chapel Hill: University of North Carolina Press.
The Life of Lazarillo de Tormes His Fortunes and Adversities. 1959. Harriet de Onís, trans. Woodbury, N.Y.: Barron's Educational Series.
Montemayor, Jorge de. 1989. *The Diana*. RoseAnna M. Mueller, trans. Lewiston, N.Y.: Edwin Mellen.

Books and Articles Cited

Abrams, Fred. 1969. "A Note on the Mercedarian Friar in the *Lazarillo de Tormes*." *Romance Notes* 11:444–46.
Alborg, Juan Luis. 1974. *Historia de la literatura española*, vol. II. Madrid: Gredos.
Alcalá, Angel, ed. 1987. *The Spanish Inquisition and the Inquisitorial Mind*. Boulder, Colo.: Social Science Monographs.
Alfonso, Pedro. 1969. *Disciplina Clericalis*, translated as *The Scholar's Guide* by Joseph R. Jones and John E. Keller. Toronto: The Pontifical Institute of Medieval Studies.
Asensio, Eugenio. 1967. "La peculiaridad literaria de los conversos." *Anuario de Estudios Medievales* 4:327–51.
Baena, Juan Alfonso de. 1965. *Cancionero*. José Maria Azaceta, ed. 3 vols. Madrid: C.S.I.C.
Baer, Yitzhak. 1961. *A History of the Jews of Christian Spain*. 2 vols. Philadelphia: The Jewish Publication Society of America.
Bataillon, Marcel. 1952. "¿Melancolía renacentista o melancolía judía?" In *Estudios Hispánicos: Homenaje a Archer M. Huntington*. Wellesley, Mass.: Wellesley College, 39–50.

Benassar, Bartolomé. 1981. *Inquisición española: poder político y control social*. Barcelona: Crítica.

Brenes Carrillo, Dalai. 1987. *"Lazarillo, La Ulixea,* y Anón." *Boletín de la Biblioteca Menéndez Pelayo* 63:57–104.

Cárdenas, Anthony J. 1987. Review of Nepaulsingh, *Towards a History of Literary Composition in Medieval Spain. Manuscripta* 31:116–17.

Castro, Américo. 1948. *España en su historia: Cristianos, moros y judíos*. Buenos Aires: Losada.

———. 1975. *Españoles al margen*, 2d ed. Madrid: Jucar.

———. 1960. *Hacia Cervantes*, 2d ed. Madrid: Taurus.

———. 1975. *La realidad histórica de España*, 6th ed. Mexico: Porrúa.

Cervantes, Miguel de. 1990. *El cerco de Numancia*. Robert Marrast, ed. Madrid: Cátedra.

Covarrubias, Sebastián de. 1943. *Tesoro de la Lengua Castellana o Española*. Martín de Ríquer, ed. Barcelona: Horta.

Creel, Bryant L. 1981. *The Religious Poetry of Jorge de Montemayor*. London: Tamesis.

Daichman, Graciela S. 1988. Review of Nepaulsingh, *Towards a History of Literary Composition in Medieval Spain. Envoi* 1:155–59.

Deyermond, Alan D. 1975. *Lazarillo de Tormes: A Critical Guide*. London: Grant and Cutler.

Diccionario de Autoridades. 1963. Facsimile edition. 3 vols. Madrid: Gredos.

Dunn, Peter N. 1990. "A Post-Modern Approach to the Spanish Renaissance: Paul Julian Smith on the Literature and Literary Theory of the Golden Age." *Bulletin of Hispanic Studies* 62:165–75.

———. 1989. "Reading the Text of *Lazarillo de Tormes*." In *Studies in Honor of Bruce W. Wardropper*, Dian Fox, Harry Sieber, and Robert ter Horst, eds. Newark, N.J.: Juan de la Cuesta, 91–104.

Epstein, Louis M. 1967. *Sex Laws and Customs in Judaism*. New York: KTAV. First published by the American Academy of Jewish Research, 1948.

Ferrer-Chivite, Manuel. 1984. "Sustratos conversos en la creación de *Lazaro de Tormes*." *Nueva Revista de Filología Hispánica* 33:352–79.

Fox, Marvin. 1990. *Interpreting Maimonides*. Chicago: University of Chicago Press.

Friedlander, M., trans. 1928. Moses Maimonides, *The Guide for the Perplexed*. London: Routledge.

Gadamer, Hans-Georg. 1975. *Truth and Method*. New York: Seabury.

García de la Concha, Víctor. 1972. "La intención religiosa del *Lazarillo*." *Revista de Filología Española* 55:243–77.

———. 1981. *Nueva lectura del Lazarillo*. Madrid: Castalia.

Gericke, Philip O. 1988–89. "Mena's *Laberinto de Fortuna:* Apocalypse Now?" *La Corónica* 17:1–17.

Gesenius, William. 1898. *Hebrew Grammar*. E. Kautzsch, ed.; G. W. Collins, trans.; 26th ed. revised by A. E. Cowley. Oxford: Clarendon Press.

Gilman, Stephen. 1972. "Matthew V:10 in Castilian Jest and Earnest." *Studia Hispanica in Honorem R. Lapesa*, I. Madrid: Gredos, 257–65.

Gómez-Martínez, José Luis. 1975. *Américo Castro y el origen de los españoles: historia de una polémica*. Madrid: Gredos.

Gómez-Moriana, Antonio. 1984. "Autobiografía y discurso ritual: Problemática de la confesión autobiográfica destinada al tribunal inquisitorial." *Zagadnienia Rodzajów Literackich* 27:5–23.

Góngora, Luis de. 1961. *Polifemo*. Dámaso Alonso, ed. 2 vols. Madrid: Gredos.

―――. 1987. *Soledades*. John Beverley, ed. Madrid: Cátedra.

―――. 1965. *The Solitudes*. E. M. Wilson and Willis Barnstone, eds. New York: Las Américas.

Greenia, George D. 1988. Review of Nepaulsingh, *Towards a History of Literary Composition in Medieval Spain*. *Hispania* 71:76–77.

Guillén, Claudio, ed. 1966. *Lazarillo de Tormes* and *El Abencerraje*. New York: Dell.

―――. 1971. *Literature as System*. Princeton: Princeton University Press.

Gutwirth, Eleazar. 1990. "From Jewish to *Converso* Humour in Fifteenth-century Spain." *Bulletin of Hispanic Studies* 68:223–33.

Halkin, Abraham, and Hartman, David. 1985. *Crisis and Leadership: Epistles of Maimonides*. Philadelphia: The Jewish Publication Society of America.

Handelman, Susan A. 1982. *The Slayers of Moses*. Albany: State University of New York at Albany Press.

Hebreo, Leon (also known as Judah Abravanel and Léon Hébreu). 1929. *Dialoghi d'Amore*. Santino Caramella, ed. Bari: Laterza.

Hébreu, Léon. 1974. *Dialogues d'amour*. Pontus de Tyard, trans.; T. A. Perry, ed. Chapel Hill: University of North Carolina Press.

Hirsch, E. D. 1967. *Validity in Interpretation*. New Haven: Yale University Press.

Homer. *The Odyssey*. 1975. Richmond Lattimore, trans. New York: Harper & Row.

Hoy, David Couzens. 1978. *The Critical Circle: Literature, History, and Philosophical Hermeneutics*. Berkeley and Los Angeles: University of California Press.

Imperial, Micer Francisco. 1977. *"El dezir a las syete virtudes" y otros poemas*. Colbert I. Nepaulsingh, ed. Madrid: Clásicos Castellanos.

Jammes, Robert. 1967. *Etudes sur l'oeuvre poétique de Don Luis de Góngora y Argote*. Bordeaux: Féret.

Kamen, Henry. 1965. *The Spanish Inquisition*. New York: New American Library.

Lang, Berel. 1990. *Act and Idea in the Nazi Genocide*. Chicago and London: University of Chicago Press.

―――. 1983. *Philosophy and the Art of Writing*. Lewisburg, Pa.: Bucknell University Press.

―――. 1993. Review of Marvin Fox, *Interpreting Maimonides*. *Judaism* 42:250–54.

Lea, Henry Charles. 1906. *A History of the Inquisition of Spain*. 4 vols. New York: Macmillan.

————. 1887. *A History of the Inquisition of the Middle Ages.* 3 vols. New York: Harper.

López Grigera, Luisa. 1976. "Un nuevo códice de los *Proverbios Morales* de Sem Tob." *Biblioteca de la Real Academia española* 56:221–81.

Maimonides, Moses. 1928. *The Guide for the Perplexed.* M. Friedlander, trans. London: Routledge.

————. 1985. *Epistles.* A. Halkin and D. Hartman, eds. Philadelphia: The Jewish Publication Society of America.

Malkiel, Yakov. 1952. "La familia *lazerar, laz(d)rar, lazeria.*" *Nueva Revista de Filología Hispánica* 6:210–76.

Manuel, Juan. 1969. *Conde Lucanor.* José Manuel Blecua, ed. Madrid: Clásicos Castalia.

Márquez, Antonio. 1980. *Literatura e Inquisición en España, 1478–1834.* Madrid: CSIC.

Marx, Alexander. 1944. *Studies in Jewish History and Booklore.* New York: Jewish Theological Seminary.

Menéndez Pidal, Ramón. 1980. *Reliquias de la poesía epica Española.* Madrid: Gredos.

————. 1983. *La leyenda del abad don Juan de Montemayor.* Dresden: Gesellschaft für romanische Literatur.

Minter, Gordon. 1987. "Some Thoughts on the Fearful Lack of Symmetry in the *Lazarillo de Tormes,*" in *A Face Not Turned to the Wall: Essays on Hispanic Themes for Gareth Alban Davies,* C. A. Longhurst, ed. Leeds: University of Leeds, 51–66.

Moreno Baez, Enrique. 1959. "The Theory of Love in the Two Dianas: A Contrast." *Bulletin of Hispanic Studies* 36:65–79.

Nepaulsingh, Colbert I. 1980. "Lazaro's Fortune." *Romance Notes* 20:1–7.

————. 1986. *Towards a History of Literary Composition in Medieval Spain.* Toronto: University of Toronto Press.

————. 1987. "In Search of a Tradition, Not a Source for *San Manuel Bueno, mártir.*" *Revista Canadiense de Estudios Hispánicos* 11:315–30.

————. 1989. "Mestureros." *Anuario Medieval* 1:156–66.

Netanyahu, Benzion. 1966. *The Marranos of Spain From the Late XIVth to the Early XVIth Century According to Contemporary Hebrew Sources.* New York: American Academy for Jewish Research. Reprint, Millwood, N.Y.: Kraus, 1973.

Norton, F. J. 1966. *Printing in Spain 1501–1520.* Cambridge: Cambridge University Press.

Núñez de Reinoso. 1944. *Los amores de Clareo y Florisea.* Madrid: Atlas, Biblioteca de Autores Españoles, III, 431–68.

Pelikan, Jaroslav. 1974. *The Christian Tradition: A History of the Development of Doctrine. Volume II: The Spirit of Eastern Christendom (600–1700).* Chicago: University of Chicago Press.

Perry, Theodore Anthony. 1969. "Ideal Love and Human Reality in Montemayor's *La Diana.*" *Publications of the Modern Language Association of America* 84:227–34.

Philo Judaeus. 1950. *The Life of Moses.* H. A. Wolfson, trans. Cambridge, Mass.: Harvard University Press.

Pinto Crespo, Virgilio. 1983. *Inquisición y control ideológico en la España del siglo XVI.* Madrid: Taurus.

Prescott, William H. 1893. *History of the Reign of Ferdinand and Isabella, the Catholic.* 3 vols. Philadelphia: McKay.

Rhodes, Elizabeth. 1992. *The Unrecognized Precursors of Montemayor's Diana.* Columbia: University of Missouri Press.

Rohland de Langbehn, Regula. 1987. Review of Nepaulsingh, *Towards a History of Literary Composition in Medieval Spain. Journal of Hispanic Philology* 11:179–81.

Rojas, Fernando de. 1985. *Celestina.* 2 vols. Miguel Marciales, ed. Urbana and Chicago: University of Illinois Press.

Round, Nicholas G. 1991. Review of Nepaulsingh, *Towards a History of Literary Composition in Medieval Spain. Bulletin of Hispanic Studies* 68:316–17.

Ruiz, Juan. 1972. *Libro de Buen Amor.* R. S. Willis, ed. Princeton: Princeton University Press.

Sánchez Ferlosio, Rafael. 1974. *Las semanas del jardín.* Madrid: Nostromo.

San Pedro, Diego de. 1971. *Cárcel de Amor* in *Obras Completas,* II. Keith Whinnom, ed. Madrid: Castalia.

———. 1979. *Arnalte y Lucinda* in *Obras Completas,* I. Keith Whinnom, ed. Madrid: Castalia.

Shem Tov de Carrión. 1986. *Proverbios Morales.* T. A. Perry, ed. Madison, Wisc.: Seminary of Medieval Studies.

Shipley, George A. 1978. "La obra literaria como monumento histórico: el caso del *Abencerraje.*" *Journal of Hispanic Philology* 2:103–20.

———. 1982. "The Critic as Witness for the Prosecution: Making the Case against Lázaro de Tormes." *Publications of the Modern Language Association of America* 97:179–94.

Sieber, Harry. 1978. *Language and Society in La Vida de Lazarillo de Tormes.* Baltimore: The Johns Hopkins University Press.

Sigüenza y Góngora, Carlos de. 1984. *Los infortunios de Alonso Ramírez.* J. S. Cummins and Alan Soons, eds. London: Tamesis.

Simón Díaz, José. 1971. "Algunas censuras de libros." *La bibliografía: conceptos y aplicaciones,* Barcelona, 269–308.

Smith, Colin. 1961. "La musicalidad del *Polifemo.*" *Revista de filología Española* 44:139–66.

Smith, Paul Julian. 1988. *Writing in the Margin: Spanish Literature of the Golden Age.* Oxford: Clarendon.

Snow, Joseph P. 1987. Review of Nepaulsingh, *Towards a History of Literary Composition in Medieval Spain. Choice* (September), 134.

Strauss, Leo. 1952. *Persecution and the Art of Writing.* Glencoe, Ill.: The Free Press.

Trachtenberg, Joshua. 1939. *Jewish Magic and Superstition.* New York: Behrman.

Unamuno, Miguel de. 1979. *San Manuel Bueno, mártir.* Mario J. Valdés, ed. Madrid: Cátedra.

Valdés, Mario J. 1982. *Shadows in the Cave.* Toronto: University of Toronto Press.

Walsh, John K. 1988. Review of Nepaulsingh, *Towards a History of Literary Composition in Medieval Spain. Speculum* 63:970–72.

———, and B. Bussell Thompson. 1983. "The Mercedarian's Shoes (Perambulations on the fourth *tratado* of *Lazarillo de Tormes*)." *Modern Language Notes* 103:440–48.

Whinnom, Keith. 1980. "The Problem of the 'Bestseller' in Spanish Golden-Age Literature." *Bulletin of Hispanic Studies* 57:189–98.

Wilson, E. M. 1973. "Inquisitors as Censors in Seventeenth-century Spain." *Proceedings of the Twelfth Congress of the International Federation for Modern Languages and Literatures*, 38–56.

Wolfson, Harry Austryn. 1938. "The Amphibolous Terms in Aristotle, Arabic Philosophy, and Maimonides." *Harvard Theological Review* 31:151–73.

———. 1962. *Philo: Foundations of Religious Philosophy in Judaism, Christianity, and Islam*. 2 vols. Cambridge, Mass.: Harvard University Press.

Woodward, L. J. 1965. "Author-Reader Relationship in the *Lazarillo del Tormes*." *Forum for Modern Language Studies* 1:43–53.

INDEX

Abravanel, Judah. *See* Hebreo, Leon

Alcalá, Angel, 15, 19

Alfonso, Pedro, 21

Allegoresis, 8–9

Almohads, 31

Aristotle, 27, 28

Asensio, Eugenio, 5

Baena, Alfonso de, 23, 137

Baer, Yitzhak: on Alfonso Espina, 19, 20; on Fray Vincent Ferrer, 90, 91; on the massacres of 1391, 22

Benassar, Bartolomé, 15

Blinding the Inquisition, ix; in *Lazarillo*, 72, 81; in *El Abencerraje*, 91–92, 96–97; in *La Diana*, 104, 110–11, 116–17; in Góngora, 128–132, 136

Blood, purity of, 115–16, 137

Borges, Jorge Luis, 6

Bread riots, 71

Breadly paradise, 71–72

Brenes Carrillo, Dalai, 46, 49–63

Cárcel de Amor: author's name in, 55, 120; as model for converso texts, 2, 6, 24, 30, 32, 33; Neoplatonic love in, 93–94, 99

Cárdenas, Anthony, 9

Castro, Américo: and converso authors, 5, 46; defines Spain's essence, ix, 2, 133

Celestina: author's name in, 53, 55, 120; as model for converso texts, 2, 24, 25, 33; Neoplatonic love in, 93–94, 99; proverbial sayings in, 137

Cervantes: as part of converso tradition, 2, 6, 33, 120, 134, 137; and the Golden Age, 130; inserts his name, 120

Circularity, in literary theory, 10, 125

Comestor, Pedro, 47

Confession, to the Inquisition, 18, 69–70; in *Lazarillo*, 38, 69–70, 78

Confesso y no nego, as joke, 48–49

Confesso, definition of, 43–44

Conquistador critics, 13, 46, 49

Consonantal patterns: in Góngora, 132, 135–36; in *Lazarillo*, 50–52; in Spanish literary theory, 128

Converso: definition of, ix, x, xi, 11–12; in dictionaries approved by the Spanish Inquisition, 42–44; in *Lazarillo*, 78; in *La Diana*, 115

Converso text: author's name in, 53, 55, 120; definition of, 2, 3–4, 5–7, 11–12, 47, 75, 104, 116–17; editing of, 133–34; theoretical underpinnings of, 14, 27–34

Covarrubias, Sebastián de, 43–44, 49

Creel, Bryant, 113

Debates, religious, 92–95, 99–101, 118–19

Derrida, Jacques, 124–25, 133

Deyermond, Alan, 123–25

Diana (the name), 110

Dissembling, 81, 117

Dunn, Peter, 46, 124

Editing. *See* converso text, editing of

Epstein, Louis M., 76

Espina, Alonso, 19–20

Ethnic cleansing, xi

Faith, religious, as love, 110, 117–19

Fernando de Antequera, 90